BEYOND OUR CONTROL

Restructuring Your Life After Sexual Assault

Leila Rae Sommerfeld

Kregel
Publications

BEYOND OUR CONTROL

To God,
the One and Only, the Creator of my being,
whose adoration for me is His magnificent
obsession. I am eternally grateful.

And to those who have suffered in silence who
are now brave enough to trust God for new
wings as He encourages us to fly beyond mere
tolerable recovery and helps us break free from
the strongholds of the past.

I will bring health and healing to [them]; I will heal my
people and let them enjoy abundant peace and security.

—Jeremiah 33:6

contents

acknowledgments

My deep appreciation to . . .

Bettie P. Mitchell, L.P.C., M.R. Founder/Director of Good Samaritan Ministries International, Beaverton, Oregon, author of *Who Is My Neighbor?* Thanks for endorsing my book and showing me what it means to be a servant of Jesus Christ.

My sisters Linda Montgomery and Gloria Griggs; my niece Lee Ann Smith; and friends Karen Hill, Ruth Morlock, Lee Ann Dillon, Edna Cooke, and Ruth Hermance for wading through the manuscript in its infancy.

Bobbie Breedlove for editing the early manuscript more times than she cared to. Her steadfast encouragement kept me going when at times I felt like a total failure.

Paulette Zubel, project editor, and Miranda Gardner, associate editor at Kregel Publications, for ironing out the wrinkles in my manuscript.

My husband, D.D., for patiently listening to my endless babble and frustrations while birthing the book. I'm sure he is delighted it's finished!

Candace Walters, author of *Invisible Wounds*, for allowing me to reprint an abundance of her writing.

Judy Boen, prison chaplain, Grover Beach, California, and Larry

Day, Ph.D., Portland, Oregon, author of *Self Esteem—By God's Design*, for graciously endorsing my book.

All the sexual assault survivors and perpetrators who shared their stories with me and gave me permission to include them in this book.

And to those who asked, "How is your book coming along?" and to those whom I have forgotten.

introduction

So I turned my mind to understand, to investigate and to search out wisdom and the scheme of things and to understand the stupidity of wickedness and the madness of folly.

—Ecclesiastes 7:25

On one single night, an intruder tore apart the fabric of my life, leaving me frozen in fear. During the summertime, more than forty years ago, I was raped in my home. My children were asleep in the next room; my husband was out of town. The rapist, I later learned, was a distant neighbor. Our home was isolated, making a prompt rescue impossible.

That act of violence left me shattered for years. More than three decades passed in silence before that fear melted. Although I received emergency medical care right after the rape, in the years that followed I failed to receive the medical, mental, emotional, and spiritual help that could have spared me decades of sorrow. My marriage dissolved. I suffered a mental breakdown, and fear held me hostage. Anxiety, panic attacks, depression, and numerous other dysfunctions followed, leaving me with a hardened heart and a hostile, embittered attitude.

I eventually came to the brink of suicide and begged God for peace—whether in life or in death. God heard, and He responded one day with an everlasting promise: *I will bring peace to your life like the calm on the morning pond.*

My journey to wholeness included interaction with perpetrators in an abuse recovery group at Good Samaritan Ministries, a Christian nonprofit mental health clinic. Many of the perpetrators were ex-convicts on parole. As I listened to their stories, my hatred and disdain toward men turned to forgiveness and compassion.

Part 1 is my story. Everyone has a story to tell, and everyone needs to be heard. In telling our stories, silence is broken and we are given a voice. Storytellers and listeners connect through a common thread—for the storyteller, healing deepens, and for the listener, healing perhaps begins. This is why I share my story. This is why I hope that someday you'll have the courage to share yours.

Within my story are stories of others—rape survivors and perpetrators. Their stories are about discovery and forgiveness, and how lives intertwine.

Part 2 of this book is divided into several short chapters covering such topics as fear and loss of safety, depression, shame and guilt, memories, where God is in the midst of your ordeal, victim thinking, and signs of healing. I suggest you read the book cover-to-cover. You may, however, skip around, choosing a chapter according to your mood or need of the day.

In the back of the book are appendixes that provide helpful resources. They are for survivors, friends, family, husbands, fathers, pastors, social workers, and counselors. Suggested reading material is also listed to help further your healing journey.

While our pain leaves wounds, you'll see that our scars can bear witness to God's unfailing love. He can create new life in you. You, too, can find healing and peace in this beautiful, savage world.

Awesome blessings!

PART 1

MY STORY

The Intruder

How was I to know that, before the dawn,
my life would forever be changed,
that the safety I once felt inside my fortress
would be shattered into splintered glass
cutting deep into my soul, leaving mortal pain,
carving fear into my heart.

You, stranger in the night, intruding into my very being,
consuming all my peace, crushing my spirit,
filling me with terror—

I will never be the same.

—Leila

chapter 1

Nighttime intruder

CORONA, CALIFORNIA, SUMMER 1963

John F. Kennedy died that year. I died a little that year too; I was raped. My rape occurred before 911 emergency numbers, rape crisis centers, and trauma counselors. I didn't dare discuss it with anyone for fear of ridicule, disbelief, shame, and embarrassment. Fear like I had never encountered became my constant shadow, and trust was a word cancelled from my senses.

The day it happened had been stifling, but the heat was cooling down as the beautiful, clear day came to a close. It was warm and muggy inside my home, making me feel like a sticky bun. The swamp wheezed cool, damp air around my bare legs as I opened the bedroom windows and checked on our sleeping girls, aged three and six. I went to the garage to retrieve a load of dry laundry, took it to the bedroom, and tossed it on the bed. Thirsty for a cool drink, I padded to the kitchen to see what I could find. As I reached for a soda, the blast of cold air from the refrigerator felt delicious.

Later, folding clothes in the peaceful silence, I let my mind wander with thoughts of the coming week. My husband, Jack, had gone to Mexico with my father to pick up a car. He was driving the car home and wouldn't be back until after midnight. Darkness closed in as the clock struck ten.

Without warning, the lights went out.

Okay, Leila, I assured myself. *So the lights went out—don't panic. Why do these things always happen when I'm alone?*

I got the flashlight and went to check the power box, hoping I wouldn't encounter a tarantula or rattlesnake.

Looking back, I wish that had been the only encounter I would have.

I'd just started for the garage when I thought I heard a noise. I stopped, stood very still, and listened. Maybe it was my imagination. No, there it was again, the sound of feet crunching gravel on our walkway. My heart beat fast as I flew to the telephone and dialed the operator.

"Someone's trying to break into my home. I'm alone with my children. Get me the police. Hurry!"

While I waited on hold, the intruder banged wildly on the front door, then on the back door. Windows rattled, and doors shook as if vibrated by thunder. I trembled with terror. He continued pounding the doors like a wild beast, unconcerned about the noise. And why should he? Our house was so isolated, who would hear? The kenneled dogs barked outside, adding more noise. I was afraid the girls would wake up.

"Corona police," announced a sleepy voice through the phone.

I quickly told him what was happening.

"I'm sorry, but you're in the county's jurisdiction. You'll have to call the sheriff."

"No!" My heart sank.

Why couldn't they put the call through for me? *God, please help!*

The operator had stayed on the line, and she'd heard his reply. So she put me through to the sheriff. I repeated what was happening and tried to give coherent directions to our home. It was hard to locate after dark—no street lights, just a few landmarks enclosed in the black of night.

The sheriff promised to come right over. I knew he wouldn't make it in time—in time for what? Robbery? Rape? Murder? I laid the phone down without hanging up. I guess having the phone off the hook helped me feel connected to the outside world.

Panic set in. I felt defenseless against this unseen enemy. I ran to the bedroom closet and took our gun from the shelf.

"I have a gun, and I'll use it," I shouted at the intruder. My voice sounded weak and unthreatening. "You'd better get out of here. I've called the sheriff."

His erratic banging didn't stop.

I decided to fire a warning shot. The gun felt smooth and cool in my sweating hand as my finger curled around the trigger and squeezed. But nothing happened! I tried again—nothing!

I felt hopeless and helpless. The intruder probably thought I was bluffing. He was in control and he knew it.

*   *   *

What had been the location of my dreams was now part of my nightmare. I'd wanted horses, and we needed property we could afford. The five-acre parcel filled the bill. We'd built a modest house, erected a small barn, put in fences, and planted a few trees and shrubs.

Our house sat on a high hill, and absorbed heat on its pale yellow, stucco walls like a painted lady butterfly sunning itself. With mountains rising to the south, and a 360-degree view, we could see for miles. Surrounding the house were rolling hills, valleys, ravines, and acres and acres of orange groves. When the orange trees were in blossom, and the breeze just right, their intoxicating scent saturated the air.

A few houses dotted the hills below. And while I occasionally saw someone wave, I never heard them.

I loved the privacy of this location, but the drive to town was about eight miles. The rutted dirt road to our home was about a half mile off a paved service road, and the hill so steep, visitors wondered if they'd drop off the edge at the summit.

We had frequent power outages, but we didn't mind. Candles, flashlights, and an occasional fire in the fireplace made the outages seem like celebrations. Besides, the power was never off for long.

But on this night, when the lights went out, there was no celebration. The most hideous, life-altering experience was about to occur, leaving my mind, body, and spirit forever changed.

*   *   *

My fear mounted as I stood in the middle of the house, shaking. I didn't know what to do except pray.

In the flash of a second, the evil intruder sprang at me from out of nowhere. He yanked my head back by my hair. His arm flew around my neck, and then he grabbed the gun from my hand.

My free hand swung around, briefly illuminating his face with the flashlight. I didn't recognize him.

He threw the gun on the sofa, seized the flashlight, and twisted my arm behind my back. Then he pushed me toward the bedroom and said, "Don't fight, and you won't get hurt."

Did I know this evil man? I wasn't sure. But he apparently knew me—from where?

Please, dear God, don't let the girls get up. I not only feared for their lives; I didn't want this horrible scene etched forever in their memory.

"Take off your clothes," he demanded.

My eyes swelled with tears as I started to unbutton my blouse.

Because I didn't want the girls to hear anything, I offered no resistance. I did as I was told, though I made no effort to be an obliging participant.

He only spoke to give me orders. He didn't talk at all during the assault. I failed to recognize him or his voice.

As I lay there enduring this monster's attack, the dogs stopped barking. The house became strangely quiet. The silence was broken by one of my daughters shouting, "Mother!"

"It's all right, honey," I replied, forcing my voice to sound calm. It's strange that I remember thinking, *I wonder if the noise woke her or the sudden silence.* Though my lips quivered, I managed to sound normal. "Go back to sleep." Miraculously, she did as she was told.

After the assault, the man stood, zipped his pants and said, "Get me your purse!"

Sitting up, my mind felt hazy and I drew a blank. "I can't remember where it is."

"Well, you'd better remember, and quick!"

Shivering from cold and shock, I wandered around the house naked with the man trailing behind me. I tried to remember where I'd put my purse, but all I could think about was whether the girls and I would be murdered.

When I finally found the purse, he seized it, and then ran out the back door.

I immediately locked the door, not realizing he had climbed in through a bedroom window. I went to my bedroom, put on a robe, then grabbed a towel from the bathroom and wiped my legs. Frightened that he would return and kill all of us, I got the girls up and made a bed for them in the bathtub. I don't remember the reason I gave them; they just climbed in dutifully and soon fell asleep—another miracle.

Fear gripped me, so great I can not describe it. I locked the bathroom door and watched out the tiny window for the lights of the sheriff's car, praying he would hurry. I felt like a character in a horror movie. This couldn't be happening to me. It must be a dream. Surely I would wake up soon.

But it wasn't a dream. It was a living nightmare.

Finally, I saw car lights, flashing up and down, back and forth like searchlights. Though I knew it was the sheriff, I felt apprehensive about opening the front door. How could I be sure it was safe?

I crept to the living room and peered out the window, straining my eyes to make out the figure stepping onto the porch. He held a flashlight in one hand and a gun in the other.

I slowly opened the door, feeling dirty and embarrassed, though I didn't know why. I hadn't done anything wrong.

I wanted to say, "You're too late. I've been raped. What took you so long?" I don't remember what I actually said.

The sheriff found the power box and flipped a switch that turned on the lights in the house. I felt exposed, like a freak from a sideshow.

Trembling, I let him inside and offered him a seat in the living room. Even though it was warm in the house, I felt cold and sick to my stomach. I wrapped my robe tightly around my body as I sat on the couch. I did my best to describe what had happened. The word *rape* stuck in my throat. Finally, I whispered, "He raped me."

He said I should go to the hospital for an examination and offered to take me.

"My husband is on his way home from Mexico," I explained. "I can't go until he gets here. I can't leave my children alone."

He nodded. "I understand."

"He should be home sometime after midnight."

"I'll wait until he comes home. In the meantime, you can get dressed and take the sheets off of your bed. We'll need them so the crime lab can look for semen. We'll also need the clothes you took off. Oh, and don't wash yourself."

Don't wash myself? How long do I have to live with his filth?

I moved in slow motion, gliding from room to room, collecting evidence for the crime lab and feeling like I was outside my own body.

After what seemed like an eternity, my husband, Jack, finally arrived. Sobbing, I told him what had happened. His expression revealed shock that such a horror could happen in his home.

"If I get hold of that ——, I'll kill him," he yelled, his face flushing.

I phoned a friend who lived nearby and asked her to stay with the girls while Jack and I went to the hospital. While we waited for her to arrive, I wondered, *Why didn't I call her when I first heard the attacker?* Maybe I couldn't remember her phone number in my panic. Perhaps I didn't want to lose the operator. Maybe I was just numb with fear.

We went to the hospital emergency room. The lobby was quiet and empty at 3 AM. After filling out paperwork, I was whisked into a small examination room and told to undress—again. White protective paper crinkled beneath my body as I climbed onto the examination table, and with only a skimpy gown to cover me, I felt exposed. I was alone—no nurse, no husband, no one to hold my hand. Shiny silver stirrups glared at me, and the idea of the cold metal sent shivers down my spine. Shaking, I felt I was about to be raped again.

The examining doctor talked little, his voice devoid of emotion. I spoke only when questioned. In my heart, I begged God to help me get through the whole ordeal.

After the exam, Jack led me back to the car. I curled up tight on the front seat. As we drove home in silence, the sun came up. The sky glowed with ribbons of crimson as a sliver of moon faded into the morning. I hugged a sweater close around my body as if to protect myself from further violence.

I wanted to die. That seemed ironic since, during the rape, I was afraid of being murdered. Did it matter now if I lived when part of me was already dead?

When we got home, I shuffled inside and took a shower. I then crawled into bed, and pulled the covers over my head.

Can I ever stay alone in this house again? God, how could You allow this to happen?

My husband notified my family. Nobody came to see me. I wasn't sure I wanted to see them anyway.

A detective came by later that afternoon. He asked a few questions to see if I could identify my perpetrator. Sitting at the kitchen table, he opened a large book.

"Leila, look at these pictures. Don't rush. Study them closely."

After a lengthy time of viewing the photos, I vaguely recognized one face. After pointing it out, the detective informed me that he was a distant neighbor—one with a long criminal history of sexual abuse charges.

The detective led me to the window and pointed to a house in the valley below. I'd been in that home once, to sell products to the man's mother. I remembered that he and his mother acted rather strange, and that he had a little girl about three years old. Poor child. Who knows what he had done to her?

The detective asked if I'd be willing to take a polygraph test. The question took me by surprise. Couldn't he tell by the way I looked and sounded that I was telling the truth? Wasn't the rape exam enough?

Feeling more like a criminal than a victim, I consented. I didn't have anything to hide. After the detective left, I crawled back into bed and covered my head again.

Retreating from the outside world, I wanted only darkness. In the mornings after Jack left for work, I buried myself under the covers. But as I tossed and turned, sunlight would peek in, coaxing me to get up. Maybe when the rapist was arrested, convicted, and sentenced, I could rise out of the rubble of my life and piece it back together.

The silence one morning was broken by the ringing of the phone. Expending all the energy I could muster, I climbed out of bed and answered it.

"Hello."

"You little tramp!" a shrill voice crackled.

Recoiling instinctively, I suspected this was the strange mother of the rapist.

"Who is this?"

"I know your kind. I saw you at the bar."

I never went to bars!

"Everything you said about my son is a lie. You'd better watch out. And you'd better watch your girls. Leave my son alone, or you'll be sorry!"

Anger welled up inside me. How dare this woman threaten my family! I slammed down the receiver then immediately picked it up again and called the detective. He said he'd be out at once to put a wiretap on the phone.

The menacing phone calls continued day and night. This all happened long before answering machines, voice mail, or caller ID. My life was already in chaos, and now I never knew when that hateful voice would intrude.

Concerned for my children's safety, I started driving them to and from their school bus stop. Again, I haven't a clue what excuse I gave them.

Everyone who heard about the rape was eager to give me safety advice. My father suggested I buy a guard dog. My stepfather told me to purchase another gun—one without a safety latch. He said, "If you'd learned to use the gun properly, the assault might have been prevented," as if it were my fault it took place.

I knew they all were trying to be helpful—but they weren't. Their comments only added more stress to my mind, already on overload. My family had no idea the fragility of my mental state, nor did they comprehend the depth of my trauma. It was more than the rape. The fear leading up to the assault—fear for me and, more so, for my children's safety—had been overwhelming. Now I needed love, comfort, and support, not a checklist for dealing with would-be intruders.

The nightmares started soon after the assault. They occurred night after night. Like a fast-forward movie, each scene would play out the same horrifying sequence: hunt me down, chase me fast, hurt me bad, terrify me. It wasn't just one man climbing up the hill to attack me—it was an army. I was looking out the window, watching them come closer and closer, frantic about how to escape.

I'd wake up before the "encounter of the awful kind" took place. But the nightmares always left me quaking, my heart pounding in my ears. I dreaded going to bed at night, always expecting the same horror show to replay itself in my sleep.

These abhorrent dreams had other recurring themes as well—being pursued by evil, losing things or pets, being abandoned.

Abandonment, it seems, had been a recurring theme throughout my life. Feelings of abandonment had, in fact, started in my childhood. I was about three years old when my mother divorced my father for committing adultery. She remarried immediately, and the new marriage was stormy. The frequent yelling and fighting frightened me, so I'd go outside or hide, trying to be invisible.

I never formed a close relationship with my stepfather. I never crawled onto his lap or wanted him to hug me, and I never called him Daddy. Now I know why—I was afraid of him. My stepfather was unaccustomed to children, and with a high-strung wife and a demanding job with long hours, he had little time or incentive to build a relationship with his stepdaughter.

Mother experienced numerous bouts of mental illness and, over the years, had been in and out of mental hospitals. Who knows what secrets held my mother in bondage, but I was instructed never to tell her anything that might increase her neurosis. Therefore, I grew up isolated, without an aunt, grandparent, neighbor, or close friend to confide in, left to sort out my own difficulties. So as an adult, I did not—and could never—find comfort in Mother.

My birth father, Harold, never addressed the rape or the issue of my trauma. It was as if he were oblivious to my grief—or in denial. He would just rant and rave about safety, politics, and football. He, too, had a past checkered by difficulties. His family sailed from Lithuania to America when he was less than five years old, and his father died en route. His mother remarried, and his step-father committed suicide. His mother never remarried.

Father was handsome, a gifted dancer, and this led him into the arms of many women. He was married six times, and was incapable of nurturing a lasting relationship. I saw my father frequently while growing up, but it was like visiting a stranger. Other than our bio-logical connection, we seemed to have little in common, our con-versations generally about nothing.

No wonder, then, I'd hungered for a father figure most of my life. I could well identify with the words of Frederick Buechner in *Godric*: "The sadness was I'd lost a father I had never fully found. It's like a tune that ends before you've heard it out. Your whole life through you search to catch the strain, and seek the face you've lost in strangers' faces."[1]

Why, I wondered, couldn't I have a normal mother and father? I wanted a mother who would pack a picnic lunch and whisk my sib-lings and me away to the beach, a mother who would shop with me and have lunch, a mother I could confide in, whom I didn't have to nurture but who would nurture me.

I wanted a father I could count on, who would give me his ap-proval and tell me I could do anything I set my mind to. I wanted a father who would take me shopping for my prom dress and take pictures of us together. I wanted a father who would love and adore my mother all of his life, a father I could admire and respect.

I wanted a mother and father who did things together. I wanted a mother and father who did things with their children. I wanted my father and mother *together*.

When I was young, I used to console myself by saying, "It's all right. Maybe a poor relationship with my parents is good. Maybe I won't feel the pain of their passing and grieve like most people do. Maybe I won't hurt." Thinking this way enabled me to survive my isolated childhood. And while there were scattered patches of tran-quility in my early life, lingering shadows of profound loneliness, anger, and sadness darkened my path to adulthood as I continued my search for "home."

*   *   *

My rape trauma had left me so emotionally shaken that everything appeared negative and frightening. A couple of months after the rape, my husband tried to console me by taking me on a short trip to Arizona. While there we stopped to tour some underground caves. As soon as I stepped into the elevator, I sensed it was a mistake. The small car felt to me like being in an icebox. It groaned, shook, and creaked as it jerked its way down. Finally it stopped and the door opened, exposing a cold, wet wall. There was barely enough room for two people to walk beside each other. The elevator door closed and began yanking and crawling its way back up. Looking around, I felt suffocated, like a mummy in a coffin.

"Get me out of here!" I shrieked.

It seemed like an eternity before the elevator returned. My husband and I quickly stepped in and he pushed the UP button. As it hauled us back to the surface—jarring from side to side—I buried my head on my husband's chest. I didn't look up until the elevator door opened.

Fear was my shadow. I felt spied on all the time, and my gun became my constant escort. I carried it even when feeding the horses. The rapist's house was in view of our home, even though a deep ravine separated us. How convenient—he could stalk me from the privacy of his own front yard!

Unremitting agony weighed me down like boulders, crushing any positive thoughts I might have had. I felt like a time bomb of rage, tears, and fear, ready to explode at the slightest provocation.

One clear, sunny day, I drove by myself to a court hearing. I'd told my husband I'd be fine, and although I should have been feeling as nice as the weather, I wasn't. I felt cold and empty, like a marble statue. Down deep, I wanted someone to go with me, but I wouldn't ask—I didn't want to bother anyone. Self-pity, reaping the price of aloneness, brought my self-esteem about as low as it could go.

As I approached the courthouse, I turned onto a one-way street. I immediately stopped when I realized I was going the wrong way, and as I started to back up, flashing red lights blinked in my rear-view mirror. "Oh, no," I muttered.

Already nervous about the hearing, I burst into tears. I tried to explain to the officer where I was going and why.

He didn't seem to care. He just stood there—matter-of-fact and stone-faced. He proceeded to write a ticket, all the while giving me a lecture, like I was a nitwit woman who didn't pay attention while driving. I felt defeated even before I arrived at the courthouse.

I don't remember much about the rest of the day. I recall being on the witness stand, answering questions as they were fired at me, and feeling like the criminal instead of the victim. The interrogation was painful, accusing, and demeaning. It left me shaken and weary.

After the trial, the rapist was convicted and sentenced to the Atascadero State Prison for the insane. But while the threatening phone calls stopped, my apprehension did not. My state of mind actually worsened.

How I wished I could escape to someplace where I could find solace and healing. In the book *Joan of Arc: In Her Own Words*, compiled and translated by Willard Trask, Joan tells a story from her girlhood:

> Not far from Domremy there is a tree called the Ladies' Tree, and others called it Fairies' Tree, and near it there is a fountain. And I heard that those who are sick with fever drink at the fountain or fetch water from it to be made well. I have heard, too, that the sick, when they can get up,

go walking under the tree. It is a great tree, a beech. Sometimes I walked there with other girls and made garlands under the tree. I have often heard it said by old people that the fairies met there. I never saw any fairies under the tree. I have seen girls hang wreaths on the branches.

There is a wood in Domremy, called the Polled Wood; you can see it from my father's door. When I was on my journey to my King, I was asked by some if there was a wood in my country called the Polled Wood, for it had been prophesied that a maid would come from near that wood to do wonderful things. But I said, I had no faith in that.[2]

I was mentally ill, and I wanted to find the Ladies' Tree. I wanted to walk under the beautiful beech tree with its graceful branches. I wanted to hang garlands and daisy chains of restoration. I wanted to walk under the Fairies' Tree, to sing and dance with joy and be restored to the woman I was before this season of darkness. I wanted to drink from the fountain of wellness and quench my thirst for peace.

I also wanted to be the Maid from the Polled Wood, coming to do wonderful things. But like Joan of Arc, I, too, had no faith in that. My faith was shattered. Not in God, at least not completely, but in humankind. Whom could I trust? To whom could I turn? Who cared? I was in a fight for survival all by myself—or so I thought. The future held the healing. Time and God had much to teach me—but I would have to wait. The journey to wellness proceeded at a snail's pace.

Many days I sat on the hillside in my yard, with my head buried in my lap, crying for hours. My husband would silently stroll past, but he rarely reached out to console me. I wondered what he was thinking. Did he think I should be getting better and getting on with my life? Perhaps he thought I was just a crybaby. Maybe he just felt helpless. I didn't know. I only knew I was losing control of my emotions.

With feelings of hopeless abandonment, I slept too much and cried relentlessly. I wanted to run away and hide.

Abandoned

I looked around. My spirit longed to share
my hurt with someone. Blackness gripped my life
as I slipped away, sinking into a bottomless pit.
Some heard me, but didn't listen.
Mother, lost in her own abyss.
Father lectured; others whispered.
"Help! Does anyone care?"
He silently passes by my tears.
Abandoned, I cry. No one hears.

—Leila

chapter 2

Nutcracker suite

CORONA, CALIFORNIA, FALL 1969

My rape trauma tore at the seams of my marriage, ripping it into pieces. My relationship with my husband wasn't smooth before the rape, and it worsened after. I had become a tyrant. I was on edge, defensive, and impatient. I put up walls of resistance. I felt angry, and nobody seemed to care. In general, I was a mess. My emotions were out of control. My depression had smothered any fire left in our marriage.

As a child, I told myself I'd never get a divorce. To me divorce was a horrific event, like a death in the family. But my childhood vow was forgotten in light of my emotional distress, and I filed for divorce.

Now my shame was compounded, and as a result, I avoided my church. I withdrew from my longtime friends, and my family. I was miserable, and the children heartbroken.

I moved out of the house with the girls, got a job in a business office, and tried to start a new life. During that time, I raged. I was promiscuous, drank, and acted rude. My mouth spewed poison and contempt.

This new life, however, left me immobile and empty. I couldn't concentrate on anything and often burst into tears over nothing. Depression consumed me. Death and darkness crouched at my door with mocking voices chanting, "Suicide!" I was on a train to nowhere, and had reached the end of the tracks. I wanted to disconnect from the world, if not through death then at least into a hiding place.

I chose the hiding place. I believe my rape triggered a mental breakdown that had already been in the works. Much later I learned the term *alarm reaction state*. Rape brutally smashed my security and, in order to cope with the attack, my body went into alarm reaction state, producing high levels of hormones. Compound this by a family history of chemical imbalance, and my emotions and reasoning power slid downhill, destined to crumple at the bottom.

I wasn't insane, but my mental health was unstable. I couldn't cope in my present state of mind, and I knew I needed help. I checked into a mental hospital in Pomona, California—which I affectionately called the Nutcracker Suite—intending to stay a short while.

It felt strange to stand at the reception counter and fill out patient admittance forms for myself. I'd watched this scene acted out with my mother many times. But the play was different now. This time I was the main character.

I gazed around the lobby, and my eyes fell on a locked door marked NO ADMITTANCE. I knew once I passed through that door, I might not exit for some time. But I didn't care. I wanted solitude, to be left alone. I didn't want to talk to anyone.

A nurse with jangling keys and shuffling feet ushered me through that ominous door. I carried nothing but a small overnight bag.

Entering my modest room, I gazed around. Compact nightstands sat beside twin beds with a privacy curtain separating them. A dark cavity of a window yawned on the opposite wall.

My days were scheduled routines—early breakfast, then the nurse's station for my ration of pills, some of which left me feeling like a zombie; then free time, lunch, more pills, afternoon group therapy . . . more free time, more pills, and then dinner. Day in and day out, it was always the same.

Group therapy was held in a room with a long table surrounded by chairs. The counselor and his assistant sat at each end of the table with their notebooks, ready to probe us for information. I was always defensive, sarcastic, and stubborn, leaving each meeting as empty as when I went in.

I never mingled with the other patients. There was a common room where we could watch television, but I never did. I didn't enjoy television—I couldn't concentrate, and didn't want to be with other people.

I preferred to go outside and soak in the warm sun, breathe the fresh air, and admire the garden. This was probably the best therapy I received. I'd close my eyes, think about nothing, and just listen— to the passing traffic, birds singing, the voices of people walking by on the sidewalk, the drone of an airplane, a siren in the distance, the occasional barking dog.

I missed my children and the dogs. The girls were staying with my sister in Oregon, and the dogs were with my ex-husband. Pets had always been important to me. Even in my childhood they were a life raft in churning waters. I loved them, and they loved me—unconditionally.

The days passed into weeks, the weeks into months. I felt as if I were in a holding pattern—like a plane circling the runway, waiting for clearance to land. I couldn't stay forever in my Nutcracker Suite, neither did I want to. But I needed to keep circling the runway, searching for the fragments of my life. After I found them, then maybe I could touch down and piece them together.

I wondered, *Will I ever be well again? Had I ever been well? What was it like to feel normal?* I didn't know.

Then one day, propelled by some inner drive, I knew it was time to leave the security of my cocoon. I'd received few phone calls and only two visitors. Like putrid water, I was stagnating in self-pity. So I stepped out into the real world, thinking I was ready for a solo flight.

Walking out of the hospital through the same lobby I'd entered just a few months before, I felt like my stay had been just a dream. Had I really recovered from my trauma and pain?

No. My hardened heart and negative attitude wouldn't allow me to move toward recovery. My time at the Nutcracker Suite had served only as a Band-Aid. I'd kept myself in virtual seclusion there, and while the solitude had allowed me to think, I'd avoided thinking about what I needed to truly recover. I wanted to stay angry.

My frame of mind prevented me from even considering God. If I acknowledged His presence, then I'd have to justify my resentment and bitterness to Him. I felt like a complete failure, and I figured God viewed me the same way. By this time my faith had so weakened it seemed impossible that God could still love me, let alone restore me.

After leaving the hospital, I lived for a while in a two-story house with floor-to-ceiling windows. One morning as I was looking outside, a small bird flew into the window and then dropped to the ground—either unconscious or dead. Within a split second, another bird flew to the ground, picked it up, and carried it away. The first bird had been dealt a harmful blow, and its mate could not bear to leave it. The tenderness of that moment left a lasting impression on me. If only humans were as compassionate.

I felt like that little bird after my rape. I, too, had been thrown against pain and fear and then hurled to the ground. About this time a recurring evil dream haunted me. I was being chased by people and creatures, and I sought shelter in a tall building. But the people and creatures tried to break into the building. I put numerous padlocks on the doors and windows. I wanted to go to the restroom, but there wasn't any privacy there. They peeped in through tiny openings, looking for a way in. I wanted to escape in my car, but there was a creature in it.

When awoke, I interpreted this dream as the rapist's continuing his quest, trying to destroy me through my mind. No matter what

I did to keep him away, he found ways to intrude. The malevolence I felt in this dream wounded me.

But my rapist hadn't returned after that summer night in 1963. I didn't recognize it then, but I was under attack by another enemy—Satan.

The following years held trials and errors, roads full of detours and potholes, and more lessons to be learned. As I bounced along, I didn't know a divine appointment with God was waiting ahead. I'd forgotten that His love for me is strong and everlasting.

I moved to Oregon, started going to church again, and remarried. On the outside I appeared to be coping, moving on. But on the inside I was still that fallen little bird.

Second Corinthians 4:6–8 says we are fragile jars of clay, carrying the awesome treasure of the knowledge of God's glory. Though we may feel hard pressed, persecuted, and struck down, in Christ, we will not be destroyed or abandoned. I didn't know it, but I was going to be rescued. Not by my mate, though, but by my heavenly Father. He had already tenderly lifted me up and was carrying me on His wings of love. And I was to receive a promise from Him—a promise that would come to pass and change me forever.

Broken vessel

My heart ached for so long, I thought my soul
had died. I hid inside myself, a broken vessel.
But You, O Holy One, had never left.
You healed my heart and
through the passing years
gently restored my soul.

—Leila

chapter 3

HIS Name IS Crackers

Many dreams revisited me over the years. In one of them, secret chambers of my mind replayed my past in vivid color. I traveled back in time to my birthplace—Phoenix, Arizona—to experience childhood once again.

I wandered around town, seeking out familiar places. I passed tall buildings, Indians on street corners pitching their wares, and store vendors selling cheap goods from Mexico. A few palm trees and cacti offered feeble shade as the sun blistered and scorched the dusty ground.

I even smelled the wonderful scents of the old five-and-dime store—cheap perfumes, cosmetics, baby powder, vanilla ice cream from the soda fountain, hot dogs, and buttered popcorn. The wares were just as enticing—tacky trinkets, cheesy clothing, comic books, toys, and gaudy jewelry. I wanted to be there again in real life, a little girl experiencing awe and wonder anew, soaking in the simplicity of that era.

As I walked the streets, a little girl appeared at my side. I told her I would show her the tavern my father owned when I was young. The tavern in my dream was a sidewalk bar where patrons sat on high stools and placed their orders. My father stood behind the counter, washing and drying glasses.

Because we were invisible, he couldn't see us. I felt sad. I wanted to talk to him, ask questions about his early life, and tell him I was sorry we didn't have a closer relationship.

My young friend and I went to the old movie theater. The vintage posters displayed movies of the '40s, featuring stars such as Rita Hayworth, Susan Hayword, Ava Gardner, Cornel Wilde, and Clark Gable.

Then the little girl disappeared, as suddenly as she'd appeared.

Leaving the downtown area, I drifted toward the back streets. There, I came upon a man who had robbed a bank. He had a dark complexion and a head of black, bushy hair. He pointed his gun at a crowd of people and said, "I'm going to kill all of you!"

I heard the police called him Crackers. They said he was a gangster. The crowd cowered in fear, waiting for the police to capture him.

Finally, the rapist had a name in my mind—Crackers. I learned the word is British slang for "insane." The name fit him perfectly—he went to a prison for the insane.

This was one of many dreams—some of them horrific—that haunted me for years. Satan had used my trauma as a springboard to perpetuate through these dreams more evil in my life. Yes, I was going to church again, but my soul and spirit were still deeply troubled and disturbed by negativity. While I loved God, I didn't at all understand Him or His ways, as I didn't understand my earthly father and his way. Satan used my lack of understanding to launch an attack of lies about God and humankind with all the fiery darts he possessed. And it worked—for a season.

*   *   *

BEND, OREGON, SUMMER 1995

Half asleep, I stumbled into the living room and plopped on the sofa. A heavy shroud—depression—smothered me, pressing in, trying to suffocate life from me. It followed me constantly. Once again, my emotions were like leaves in a whirlwind, tossed and scattered every which way. I knew I had to get control of them.

I cried a lot, was on edge, and just wanted to be left alone. I might as well have been in another room when conversing with others. Their voices were strange, colorless. I'd look into their faces, hear the drone of their words, but I was unable to comprehend what they were saying. I just wanted to escape. I struggled to repress intruding thoughts, but they absorbed me. I kept thinking, *I've got to get out of here!*

By this time I'd learned a lot about mental illness, and I knew that the chemical imbalance in my brain was getting dangerously out of control. I needed more help than I could give myself. I needed a doctor—again.

God, I've tried so hard. I have nothing left to give. Help me!

I was sitting on the sofa, staring out the window, past the deck, the lawn, and the juniper trees. I gazed transfixed upon the pond; it was beautiful. A lone goose paddled through the morning mist, etching a lazy V-shape through the still water. I sat in silence, listening for God to respond to my plea.

Then, like a ticker tape flashing through my mind, a thought came: *I will bring peace to your life like the calm on the morning pond.*

I sat there dumbfounded, not quite believing what I'd heard.

The thought came again: *I will bring peace to your life like the calm on the morning pond.*

I wasn't imagining it. It was loud and clear in my head. God had spoken.

I dragged myself to the edge of the sofa and leaned forward. *You will? Okay, I can wait another day—what have I got to lose. Only my life.*

I didn't know how God was going to bring peace into my life, but I knew if He said He would, He would. He had the perfect plan for my future—if I didn't get in His way. Controlling my emotions and waiting patiently would be another test of fire. I sighed, lay down, and fell asleep.

The days passed, some wrinkled and some smooth. I accepted the smooth ones with gratitude and tried not to question the wrinkled ones. My doctor prescribed an antidepressant to correct the chemical imbalance and, theoretically, cure my depression. I was desperate and willing to try anything for peace.

After a week, something remarkable happened. I woke up one morning, and I wasn't depressed. In fact, I felt wonderful!

Amazing! And all it took was a little pill.

This must be what it's like to feel normal. I'm not crazy. Thank You, God!

At first I called my antidepressant my "crazy pill," and then later, I decided I should call it my "happy pill."

As summer progressed, I was finally beginning to enjoy life. I wasn't depressed, and I wasn't out of control. I occasionally felt fearful, though, especially at night. When my husband was out of town, I never slept in bed—always on the sofa. I kept a gun, car keys, and a flashlight beside me, ready to make a quick getaway. At times I'd sleep on the floor by the front door. I once fled with my dogs to a motel to escape overwhelming fear that flooded me. During these episodes I felt physically captive to fear, in mental torture, after all this time reliving the trauma over and over again in my mind.

One morning at the end of a church service, the visiting pastor called my husband and me to the front of the congregation. Having never met us before, he asked us a few questions. He announced that we would be celebrating something special in six months. He then pointed his finger at me and said, "You are not to be afraid of the night anymore."

I was stunned. Only God knew the depth of my debilitating nighttime fears. Surely God was telling me, through this prophetic word, that I was to be set free, once and for all. God's grace would make a way of escape for me.

Still, I questioned myself. I wondered if I would ever be able to sleep in my own bed without my husband beside me to make me feel safe.

My test of fire came all too soon. A couple of days after receiving that prophecy, my husband left on a business trip. As bedtime drew near, a thought flashed in my mind: *You can go to bed now.* Those words played around in my head as the evening wore on and I wore out.

Finally I said, "God, will You be mad at me if I don't sleep in my bed tonight? I want to, and I know Your word is true. But would it be okay if I tried tomorrow night?" I felt terrible for my cowardliness and lack of faith. Yet I also felt comforted and assured as I settled onto the couch for the night.

I kept my word the following night. After much procrastination, I crawled into bed. It felt strange and alone in the ominous, silent dark.

I drew a deep breath. "Okay, God, here I am. I'm doing my part—now You do Yours. Help me not to be afraid."

I closed my eyes, said my prayers, and tried to relax. I glanced at my Rottweiler sleeping soundly at the foot of my bed and felt some measure of comfort. Was that cheating?

The next morning I almost wept tears of joy to realize that I'd slept through the night.

I came to realize that my enemy was not merely fear. Sometimes fear is an ally, a rational response. My original fear was real and justified—when the attacker was trying to break into our home, while he was raping me, and even for a period of time after the event. But worry is not true fear. Worry is *anticipating* that something bad might happen. Worry is Satan's lies translated into fear. David wrote in Psalm 4:8, "I will lie down and sleep in peace, for you alone, O LORD, make me dwell in safety."

escape

I ran as fast as I could to escape
the black clouds that shrouded my heart
in a world without color or light.
Running, always running, in darkness.
I tried to ignore my clouded heart.
Dying slowly, hope abandoned, I poured out
my soul to the heavenly Father.
His breath of life flowed into me,
scattering the clouds, reviving my spirit,
setting me free.

—Leila

chapter 4

The Loud, Silent Year

I told myself that someday I'd write a book. Over the years I'd done some writing, published poems and articles, but nothing as daunting as a full-length book.

Then in 1996 I became an advocate with the Washington County Sexual Assault Resource Center. There, I cofacilitated classes for women in rape recovery. While the program was helpful and supportive, it frustrated me that the spiritual needs of the women were unmet. I wanted to offer a class to the women that would address their relationship with God.

Thus began the inquisition for this book. Yes, *inquisition* is the correct word, because at times the writing process felt almost like torture. After months of research, I started my first chapter—and got as far as one sentence. It was traumatic reliving every moment of my rape sentence-by-sentence. I put it aside and tried again the next day.

Writing during this time was like trying to start a cold car engine—sputtering a few words at a time. This went on for days.

Then one morning my fear seemed to disappear, and the words began to flow. As I wrote, though, I thought only of the negative effects of my rape. Still waiting for the complete peace that God had promised me, I continued to dwell on my fear, bitterness, and anger.

What was the point in sharing my story, though, if I couldn't offer rape survivors some encouragement and hope? Somehow, somewhere, there had to be *some* positive outcomes, but I just couldn't see them—yet.

After I'd completed about three-fourths of the manuscript, my writing came to an abrupt halt—again. I tried to write, but the words simply wouldn't come. I didn't seem to have any more to say. So the manuscript sat on a shelf for more than a year, collecting dust. Every time I passed the shelf, though, I felt a little twinge—not exactly guilt but a feeling that this whole book thing was unresolved. I even considered putting it somewhere out of sight.

During this time of waiting, however, a wrestling match was going on—God and I over my self-will. And what a God of mercy we have. He finally pierced my spirit, making me a poster child for His grace. My rebellion eventually gave way, and I yielded myself to God, trusting that whatever took place would be His will; more words would come—or they wouldn't. The writing would be left as is—or the story completed. I never exhausted Him of His love and patience for me. I had to keep putting aside my will, allowing me to become teachable, allowing me to hear Him speak.

What I thought was a silent year, was actually one of the most profound years of my life. God spoke, and—for a change—I listened. If I was to find healing in the present, I had to engage the past with an open heart and push aside disappointments and sorrow. I had to trust God.

Finding healing in the way God intended would lead me to discover myself in a whole new way. That discovery did not occur step-by-step, in neat sequence, but in writing this book, I realized healing was primarily about two things: attitudes and forgiveness. Trevor Hudson wrote that attitudes are the way we perceive reality.[1] My traumas are a reality, a *fact*: my parents' problems left me to fend for myself; as an adult I had been assaulted and wounded; after my rape, some people said and did unwise things in my presence.

In Liberty Savard's book *Shattering Your Strongholds*, she says, "Something traumatic happens in my life which is a *fact* which leads me to develop a *wrong* pattern of thinking—which helps me *justify* a wrong behavior which causes me to erect strongholds to protect my right to do so, which perpetuates my pain by keeping the trauma locked in and God locked out."[2]

My traumas led me to develop wrong patterns of thinking about my own realities, which led to attitudes like contempt for life and blaming others. I had hardened my heart, allowing God in only as I felt like it. In their book *Christ-Centered Therapy*, Neil Anderson, Terry Zuehlke, and Julianne Zuehlke say, "[Attitudes] are buried deep in our minds and they are what keep people in bondage to the past, not the traumatic experience itself."[3]

What makes a difference in our attitudes is our perception of the traumas. I'd perceived my parents' behavior as deliberate abandonment of me, my rape as evidence that God didn't love me, unkind words and acts as done with intent to hurt me. This wrong thinking led to blaming others as a way to justify my rebellion. I believed I had the right to do as I pleased even if it meant hurting others.

Blaming as a defense mechanism for one's own bad behavior dates back to the garden of Eden. Adam blamed Eve—and even God for giving her to him—and Eve blamed the serpent. This was the beginning of the blame game, and we as humans still often blame others for our sin and poor decisions.

I had not allowed a teachable spirit or a forgiving heart to develop in me. This is rebellion toward God, and I needed to repent of it. I could not continue to hang on to past wounds as an excuse to justify my anger, rage, and bitterness. What purpose would it serve? I needed to deal with the past in a different way I couldn't undo the reality of events, but with God's power, I could change the way I perceived those events.

Over that loud, silent year, I realized that my parents had not deliberately abandoned me, but had lived their lives the only way they knew how. When my father was alive he was never at peace, a man unfulfilled, seeking happiness in all the wrong places. I know now it was because he left God out of his life.

This new perception allowed me to repent of my resentment toward them. I could recognize that my rape occurred not because God didn't love me, but because evil exists in this world. I began to accept that all men are not evil, only the ones with evil intent. I accepted that what others said and did after my rape were not intended to pile on to my trauma, but merely a result of their own defense mechanisms.

Once my perceptions changed, I began to understand the effects of my old, negative attitudes. It's dangerous to believe we will never suffer the consequences of a hardened heart. Consequences are what usually change our behavior, and the ugly consequences of my behavior led me to positive changes.

Those changes had been a long time in coming, and in the process some serious spiritual warfare was waged. When the psyche has been deeply wounded, Satan marches in and launches a battle for the soul. His favorite weapon is lies—lies about you, about your relationships, about God. Satan used my negative encounters with men to influence my perception of them. This produced in me a hostile, suspicious attitude of all men. I'd let Satan's lies lead me into prideful contempt, which in turn only fed my own victimization. Another of Satan's weapons is thievery. He tried to steal my hope for the future by reminding me of lost dreams, failures, betrayals, and traumas. I realized I'd become partners with the Evil One in my own suffering.

I needed to forgive. I'd sensed this for some time, but couldn't quite figure out what it meant to forgive. What, exactly, is the Christian meaning of forgiveness? And *how* do I forgive?

The answer is, *I* can't—at least not at the human level, with my own will and intellect. Because I'd been unwilling to forgive, God overwhelmed me with the truth that we need His power to forgive.

As I listened to God, the perception of my past began to change. In turn, my past attitudes changed. I was not about to thank the rapist or others who had turned my world upside down, but because of them, I was forced to look deep inside myself. I had been licking my wounds for years, and now it was time to face the truth and be set free. Weary from a sorrowful heart, I relented and repented.

Because of God's grace, my series of unfortunate events did not destroy me. Instead, they eventually led to repentance, redemption, and a calling from God on my life. This book is part of that calling, and in part 2 I discuss more deeply the topics of coping and forgiveness. For right now, know that God has not given up on you. I'm thankful He never gave up on me. Once the old battle within began to cease, a new path to victory through Christ began.

voices

I thought I heard voices from the playhouse,
but when I looked, no one was there.
I turned to leave, when again I heard
 a far-away song, oh so fair.
I stood very still and strained to hear
a tune from olden times.
Memories returned of children singing
Sunday school songs and nursery rhymes.

—Leila

chapter 5

Facing the Enemy

Corona, California, Summer 2005

My eyes strained to see the "painted lady" on the hilltop. She was still there, the pale yellow house hiding behind tall trees that had been planted more than thirty-five years ago.

Like a victim returning to the scene of the crime, I went for a face-off where my rape, divorce, and mental breakdown had taken place. Feeling liberated from past traumas, I wanted to confront my emotions. Had I honestly recovered?

I also wanted to return to the mental hospital and look at my medical records. The hospital would be a challenge to find, as I had no idea where it was. I didn't even remember the name of the institution.

My children cautioned me not to make the journey, saying I'd be sad and disappointed. I should just remember the old place like it used to be. "Besides," they said, "unpleasant memories could surface, perhaps setting you back."

Certain in my plans, and hoping my children would be proven wrong, I continued with the venture. My niece Vicki agreed to take a day off from work and join me. Locating the old house was easy. But it looked different. Everything seemed dry, dirty, and bleak. The old horse corrals and barns were gone, as well as a couple of neighboring homes. A few new ones dotted the landscape.

"Vicki, I heard that a strange single man now lives in the house. Maybe it's my perpetrator," I teased. "You should go to the door first."

"That's fine with me," she said. "I'm not afraid of anyone."

Slowly, we got out of the car and, advancing only a few feet at a time, looked around. Trees, shrubs, and flowers grew where there was once bare ground. We stole glances through the windows, curious to see, but afraid of who might appear. Even though a truck sat in the driveway, nobody came to the door when we knocked. Old shovels leaned against the front door, along with well-worn rubber boots and a couple of buckets.

Strange, I thought. *Why would anybody need rubber boots in this hot, dry place? Maybe they're worn to prevent rattlesnake bites.*

I searched the valley below for the enemy's house. It was gone— vanished along with the perpetrator, his daughter, and his mother. I wondered about them. Was the daughter happy? Was the mother dead? Where was he? What evil spirit held that family in bondage?

Wandering off by myself to look around, I stopped first at the area that once held a playhouse for the girls. I could almost hear their piping voices and see them playing in the little house their father had built with such love and care. The dogs would be running and howling as beagles do.

I gazed at the large expanse of flat ground carved into the hillside that once was our riding arena. I saw myself training my beautiful white Arabian stallion, War Prince. Around and around he would canter, following my commands.

I saw myself riding my first Arabian mare, Rokkessa, bareback around the arena. Her damp copper coat was warm and sticky to my bare legs. She was easy to train and always obedient. She melted my heart with her beautiful dish-shaped head and large, liquid brown eyes. When she ran free, she would hold her tail high, and then stop and turn toward me, prancing, as if to say, "Look at me— I'm lovely!"

I could see the girls riding Thunder, a pokey old palomino gelding that never went faster than a walk until the day lightening struck close by. Then he lived up to his name. He ran like thunder!

I once again heard the soft nicker of the horses as I threw them hay and poured oats into their feed buckets. There was Nanny, our goat, running to catch up with me in my old, battered golf cart, and then jumping on for a ride to the bottom of the hill where other horses were waiting to be fed.

I scanned the valley below where the girls and I rode through the orange groves, up the mountain, and down the ravines. We were always watchful for rattlesnakes.

I remembered listening intently for night sounds on our intercom as Rokkessa was ready to deliver her first foal. The splash of her water breaking alerted me. I grabbed my flashlight and ran to her stall. The soft glow of light, the smell of wet straw and sweat from her laboring filled me with awe as a miracle was about to take place, the first of many to follow.

I remember the morning I came back into the house after feeding the horses and found one of the beagles had eaten a dozen donuts and half a loaf of bread. She didn't get dinner that night.

I recalled the soft chirps of baby chicks huddled together under a heat lamp as the girls and I stood by in wonder. I relived trying to grab the baby pigs that had escaped their pens and ran all over the hillside. They chased the neighbor's cows from my yard that had also escaped their pens. The cows were running fiercely to catch up with War Prince, who was eager to get to the mares. He, too, had escaped his pen.

What wonderful chaos!

I began to mourn. I mourned the life I would never have again—exciting moments with the animals, treasured times with the girls. I mourned the loss of my first marriage. I mourned the loss of the life that once was, and never will be again.

At that moment, I wondered what my life would have been like had it not stopped at that place in time, had I not been raped. Or had someone come, put their arms around me and said, "Please Leila, don't give up. Please Leila, let me help. Let me walk with you through this. Let me pray you through this."

Maybe some did. If they did, I don't remember. Apparently, those who knew me only *thought* they knew me. They didn't recognize my increasing depression as a form of mental illness.

Sometimes recovery can take years, happening in spurts. Recover, feel good. Regress, feel bad. Recover, feel good. Regress, feel bad. On and on it goes, but it always gets better, less painful. But forty years later, I sometimes wake up, crying, wondering, *Why am I crying now?* That day at the old house, I realized my mourning wasn't complete, just buried.

My children were right; unpleasant memories did surface. What should have been pleasant memories—fun times with the animals, children, and husband—became unpleasant memories as they reminded me of what I'd lost. Yes, I was sad. Yes, I still felt angry that the rapist had disrupted our once happy life.

Yes, I'm human.

Yes, I know ugly thoughts will surface from time to time. I know I might experience an occasional meltdown—like the time, thirty years after the rape, I suddenly screamed and fell upon my husband's shoulder in the movie theater, sobbing.

We were watching *A Beautiful Mind*. It was about a schizophrenic man in a mental hospital. He was on the floor being laced into a straight jacket. His eyes pleaded, "Help me, somebody! Help me!" At that moment, *he* became *me*. Up to then, I hadn't thought much about my time in the mental hospital, or at least I didn't think I had. But something inside snapped. I needed to mourn that season of my life. After my encounter-of-the-awful-kind in the movie theater, I felt a sense of release.

I knew my God is great. He is my healer. He is my comforter. He is my hope for a better tomorrow. I knew He would continue to heal me. I stood face-to-face with my past, mourned it, and looked forward to God's purpose for my future.

Vicki and I drove down rutted dirt roads in the area, searching for familiar landmarks. The little Mexican café and beauty salon were nowhere in sight. The turkey ranch and most of the orange groves were gone. "Home" was no longer there. Things were not the same.

Arriving in town, we searched for my old hideaway—the mental hospital. The first place we found was the one. I didn't recognize the name, though. The parking lot was gone, and the building appeared smaller than I remembered.

Entering the lobby, I felt a familiar sense of belonging. The admittance counter was right where I thought it would be. After what seemed like a long time, a woman finally appeared. I introduced myself and told her my reason for being there. She gazed coolly at me, apparently uninterested in my pursuit. With the aloofness of an afghan hound, she tossed her head and said, "I'm sorry, madam, but it's against policy to let strangers wander the halls without prior permission."

"Please!" I begged. "I won't bother anyone. I only want to reacquaint myself. It will be of great benefit for my book."

She stared at me for several moments. I was about to give up trying to convince her when she motioned me to follow. I scurried through the doorway, giving her no chance to change her mind.

This time, as I followed the nurse with the jangling keys, I wasn't in a daze. I was clearheaded, drinking in all the surroundings. Yes—there was the nurse's station, just where I remember it. The pill-popping place dubbed Poppies. *Tiny,* I mused.

"Is the conference room around the corner?" I asked.

"It is, madam."

All right! I knew this was the right place.

As I walked the narrow halls on cracked linoleum floors, familiar odors floated to my nostrils. Eerie sounds—ones with which I was well acquainted—rang mournfully against the stained walls beneath dreary lighting. The outdoor patio was minimal and sparse of landscaping. I must have been really sick to think I enjoyed myself in that pitiful garden. I was probably desperate for fresh air.

Trotting hastily behind the nurse, I asked, "May I see my medical records?"

She let out a deep sigh. "I'm sorry, madam. We only keep them twenty-five years. After that, they're destroyed."

Drat! I should have made this trip five years ago.

Though her answer was disappointing, I was not discouraged. I was, however, amazed. Did I look and act like these patients when I was there? Void of expression, lifeless, slow to move? How did I endure such a dismal atmosphere for so long? It wasn't awful—just isolated and depressing. I didn't realize how sick I was then.

I had the answer to the question I came for. Had I honestly recovered? No, not completely, but I wasn't worried, because He who began a good work in me will carry it on to completion until the day of Christ Jesus (Phil. 1:6).

Had I forgiven my perpetrator? By God's grace . . . yes.

Did I still hate him? No . . . not any longer.

I journeyed to the past, mourned it, and was now ready to put the sadness behind me. I looked forward to the future with sweet anticipation.

Please Accept Me

Don't give up on me.
Please accept me for who I am
today
and how far I have come from
yesterday.
Your acceptance, love, and encouragement
gives me
strength, hope, and desire for
tomorrow.
Please don't give up on me.
God hasn't.

—Leila

chapter 6

perpetrators change—
well, some DO

Portland, Oregon, 2001

The first time I visited Good Samaritan Ministries, a nonprofit Christian mental health clinic, was more than forty years after I was raped. Sitting in on a meeting of recovering sexually assaulted women, male sex offenders, and various other criminals tested my attitude toward group therapy. After all, I was a wounded veteran of sexual assault. Who could be more authoritative about the subject than I?

My skin crawled as I listened to Joe (not his real name) recount his life of crime. Was I supposed to believe that this person—a former multiple rapist—could change? Were any of us safe around him? I glared at him as he told his story.

Lurking to the side of a hiking trail in the Columbia River Gorge, Joe patiently waited for three approaching women. They soon passed by and began to cross a creek single file. Joe seized the last woman. She struggled fiercely, screaming. When the other women joined the chorus of screams, Joe fled.

Like a whipped pup, he turned tail, got in his car, and drove a few miles to another trailhead. He waited. Soon, an old woman and a young girl wandered down the trail. Joe grabbed the girl. The woman picked up a large tree branch and vigorously hit him over and over. In spite of Joe's threats, the old woman would not give up. Again, he fled.

One sunny day on the Oregon coast, Joe sat in his car getting drunk. A station wagon with four women inside pulled up. They parked their car and began unloading an enormous amount of camping gear. Joe's mind started to race.

He drove to a secluded spot down the road, and then walked back as dusk was falling. Joe stalked the women as they set up camp in a nearby wind cave. *Perfect*, he thought as two of them headed his way. When they were close enough, he plowed into the two, knocking them to the ground. They struggled briefly, but stopped when they realized he held a gun to the head of one of them.

"Be quiet and you won't get hurt," he growled.

Pausing, he wondered what to do next. He had to think fast; the other two women were advancing toward him.

One of the two women he'd captured, a powerful-looking brunette, looked straight in his eyes and said, "What do you think you're doing?"

"I can do whatever I want since I'm the one with the gun."

Without missing a beat, the woman helped her friend up.

"Stop messing around or I'll shoot," Joe ordered.

"Get out of here and leave us alone," the woman screamed. "If you don't, I'll cram that gun right up your nose."

Confused, shocked, and dumbfounded, Joe fled—again.

But Joe persisted. And he finally met with success. Eventually he raped a woman. Then he went on to rape others. All together, his kidnappings, gun possessions, and rapes netted him an exorbitant amount of years in prison. Due to technicalities and a plea bargain, he served only a fraction of his sentence.

At the counselor's prodding, Joe told the group about his childhood. Like many perpetrators, it was miserable. Seeking friendship, he escaped his abusive home life by visiting two older men next door. They treated him well and were generous with their beer and smokes. Then one day the two guys said to the eleven-year-old boy, "We've been nice to you. Now it's time for you to pay us back."

What are they talking about? Joe wondered. He soon found out. The men raped him.

Joe didn't tell anyone for fear no one would believe him. Sadness, confusion, and dysfunctional thinking took hold. His life was changed forever.

Before being released from prison, Joe spent many months in treatment for sex offenders at a state hospital. While there he realized he had terrorized all of his victims. He vowed never to harm another woman.

His decision was dramatically reinforced when he was placed in a victim's confrontation session. Seeing so much pain on the faces of survivors caused him to remember the hours of terror he'd experienced as a youth. It made him see how ugly and hideous he had become.

Joe found his way to our abuse recovery group and began to attend regularly, submitting himself to accountability. He grew spiritually, and this reinforced his choice to change his thinking.

However, Joe usually left the group meetings early. He had a hard time sitting through an entire class. He couldn't stand to hear the painful words—they hit too close to home, both as a childhood victim and as a perpetrator. Joe was particularly moved with compassion toward a woman I'll call Sue, and when she finally got the nerve to share her story, Joe got up and left the room.

Sue grew up in an unsafe home that was always filled with violence. Her father was a mean, vicious, cruel man. Her earliest memories are of her father flying into rages and beating her mother. Soon, he began beating Sue.

As the family grew, her brothers and sister were drawn into the circle of beatings. She learned very young how to read her father's face and would react by taking her brothers and sister outside or into another room so they wouldn't get beaten. He instilled such terror in them that her little brother would wet his pants whenever their dad walked by. Many times, Sue would step up to interfere with their beatings, and she in turn received what was meant for them.

They were taught to lie about their bruises. They were taught to protect him. They lived in constant fear for their lives. When other families found out about the violence in her home, their children were not allowed to visit. As a result, Sue's childhood grew increasingly lonely. Sue even began to think that something was wrong with her.

Sue's father also sexually molested her, threatening to kill her and her mother if she told anyone. She didn't tell—until now.

When Sue first came to the abuse recovery group, she sat petrified. She trembled and cried, barely able to speak her name. Bettie, the group leader, spoke for her and held her hand throughout the entire session. Sue always positioned herself by other survivors, which made her feel safe.

In class, Sue learned that perpetrators are human and that all of them had been victims of abuse too. Their stories were so similar to her own that these people could have been one of her brothers or sister. Compassion entered her heart.

She wrote a letter to her dad, expressing grief over her childhood. But he passed away before responding to it. She read the letter to our group. After that, forgiveness filled her heart. She was free from the past, experiencing peace at last.

Joe was touched by Sue's letter. He told Sue that if her dad had lived long enough, a letter from him to her might have read something like this:

> To my daughter Sue,
>   I don't know where to begin, Sue, but I am writing this with the hope that you will finally, after so many years and

my passing, find some closure for the pain in your heart and soul that you suffered at my hands.

My Sue, so much has been shown to me since I left. I come back to you now not to further torment you, but to ask for forgiveness. This is not for me, but for you. I hope in forgiving me you will be able to someday release the pain in your life—the pain you did not deserve nor want.

Your letter caused me deep sorrow for the evil things I did to you. I didn't acknowledge the letter at that time—I couldn't. I could not face the fact that I molested you and robbed you of so much of your life. I did not deserve to have you for my daughter, nor did you deserve to have me as your father and tormentor.

Sue, I am sorry for hurting you and for never acknowledging my sins to you or validating you as a child in need. Even after you became an adult, I never validated you.

I don't expect anything I say will make things okay. No father has the right to do what I did to you. Your life will never be okay unless you find strength in the Lord.

Sue, there are many things I would take back if I could. I wish I could have been the father you needed me to be for you. I now see myself for what I am, for what I was, and for what I will always remain because I did not do anything to change while I had the chance. Now that chance is lost to me. Yet, if I could speak to you, I would tell you I was terribly wrong, terribly selfish, and terribly abusive.

My daughter, I am so very sorry. If I could pray, Sue, I would pray that you would move through the pain and leave it behind. Find joy and happiness in everything.

I must go now, my daughter. May God be with you always.

Dad[1]

Although Joe wrote this letter in place of Sue's father, I suggested to Joe that—in reality—the letter was written for all the women he had abused. He denied it, but I believe in my heart that my theory is correct.

My perception of perpetrators continued to change.

o' woman of another time

O' woman of another time, weeping, waiting
to be rescued from evil. One taste of
forbidden fruit caused the Fall,
for which the Son came to die for all.

O' weeping woman, your legions fled,
were cast into the sea. The accuser
who reviled your soul,
the Son of God did trample, and broke at last
the strongholds of your past.

O' woman of another time, endued
with peace, sheltered beneath His wings
of love. Kissed with mercy, held by grace,
someday you shall see Him face to face.

—Leila

chapter 7

Tough Love

I learned about tough love three hours at a time. That's the length of the weekly abuse recovery group at Good Samaritan Ministries where survivors and perpetrators congregated together. Talk about storm currents in the air! Rapists, pedophiles, robbers, and an assortment of other offenders (most on parole) had a chance to hear the emotional damage done to the survivors of their abuse. No thoughts, feelings, or words were held back. Survivors cried, cursed, and—eventually—some were able to forgive.

Many perpetrators were horrified at the pain they had inflicted upon others. It caused them to think differently about their crimes. For months I listened to their stories, and I was amazed!

Forgiveness from survivors came because they were able to face perpetrators and hear their own stories of horror. No, we did not excuse or condone their hideous acts of crime, but we learned what led them into their destructive lifestyle. As Gavin de Becker says in *The Gift of Fear*, "A difficult childhood excuses nothing, but explains many things."[1]

I remember a particular abuse recovery meeting where several men and women gathered, no more than a few feet apart. One woman in her late forties, whom I'll call Jennifer, had a childhood filled with the horror of sexual and satanic ritual abuse. It's incredible she didn't split into different personalities to survive the torture she endured. During the session she wore an expression of concentrated hate, fear, and defiance on her face, directed at a former rapist and ex-convict (whom I'll call Darren), who sat across the circle from her. A slender man in his early fifties, with thoughtful grey eyes, Darren explained that he had been out of prison for six years after serving seven years of a twelve-year sentence.

All sex offenders in Oregon are required by law to attend abuse recovery classes while on parole. According to Bettie P. Mitchell, founder and director of Good Samaritan Ministries, their abuse treatment program is the only one of its kind in the United States (to their knowledge). The treatment program for offenders puts them in a group with adult victims of verbal, physical, and sexual abuse. The purpose is to help offenders and victims communicate with one another and work through the long-standing resentments, emotional disfiguration, and suffering that come about from abuse and rape attacks. Darren's turnaround began when he started attending these classes.

Darren told his story of growing up as a troubled child in a home without any sense of order. He had been a small, fragile child, and his older brothers mercilessly picked on him. There was never anyone home to intervene. When he was about nine years old, the family home burned down and his parents divorced. Darren stayed with his mother, who was not home enough to fulfill her role of maternal guidance. After his mother remarried, his stepsisters exposed him to sexual play. Throughout high school, Darren lived with his father and, after graduation, he enlisted in the military. When he finished his hitch, he married his high school sweetheart, who was pregnant with another man's child. That marriage did not survive. Neither did the next one.

When Darren married his third wife, she brought three stepdaughters into the union. He had deviate sex with them, and when it was discovered, he was convicted of statutory rape and sentenced to twelve years in the state penitentiary.

While he was in prison, Darren made a decision. He chose to change his thinking and his behavior. But who could help him make this change? He felt powerless to change himself; of all addictions, sexual addiction is one of the most powerful. He wanted to be free of sexually abusive behavior, but the desire was overwhelming.

He devised mental games to avoid obsessing, but they weren't successful. Finally he begged God to take the voracious appetite from him. The very next day, he felt miraculously free of the hound that had ridden his back for years.

During his time in prison, treatment programs for sex offenders were minimal, and psychological therapy at the state hospital was almost nonexistent. Since there was no one to come to the inmates with a recovery agenda, Darren decided that they would have to help themselves. So he started a Bible study in the prison courtyard, as well as a sex offender's recovery program. It began with two men and soon grew to sixteen.

After seven years in prison, Darren was released on parole. He was required to participate in an abuse recovery group, which led him to Good Samaritan Ministries.

While Darren told his story, Jennifer could not hide the repulsion on her face. She sat on the "safe" side of the room, close to a counselor she knew, and stared at him with hate, fear, and disgust in her eyes. Finally, unable to contain her rage any longer, Jennifer screamed at him, "How could you be allowed to be in this room? You don't deserve to be here. You're not even human."

Darren stood, his eyes filled with sorrow and compassion, and stepped across the room to comfort her. She shrank from him as if he were contagious. "You terrify me. Get out of here. I can't sit in this class with you!"

Jennifer's counselor advised Darren to return to his seat. Then she convinced Jennifer to stay, and as she did, she continued to glare at him. Darren quietly concluded his story with a brief description of the rape for which he was convicted and sentenced. Then discussion was opened to all individuals in the group.

One woman asked, "Do you think group sessions like this strengthen your resolve to—you know—not sexually assault another woman again?"

"Yes, they do," Darren said slowly. "I've learned that sexually addicted people like me are hard to cure. We're like alcoholics who always have thoughts of liquor somewhere in the back of their minds. Most rapists, even those who've been convicted of sex crimes, repeat them. God helped me when there was nothing I could do to help myself. Groups like this are great for people like me, even though I know they're rough on the women who come, because they're reminded—when they look at us—of the man who did the worst thing to them they could think of."

Encouraged by the compassionate silence that filled the room, Darren continued. "Another thing that's helpful in group therapy is learning about why you did what you did. You can hear stories of others, and offenders have a chance to talk about themselves and let go of bottled-up feelings."

Perhaps the most valuable benefit of the abuse recovery group is the opportunity for offenders and victims to sit face-to-face and listen to others describe episodes of terror or reform in their lives. To hear a convicted rapist confess to his crippling sexual confusion is not only a shock and a revisitation to the terror that originally overwhelmed a victim, but vindication from self-blame as well.

This was certainly the case with Jennifer. Tough love is the path to healing, but it isn't always pleasant to participate in group therapy.

Darren had been a victim as well as an offender. He needed to be healed from his childhood pain and learn how to forgive others and himself. During the many group sessions he attended, he learned how to ask for forgiveness. He discovered more about the healing power of God and how to hold on to his life-changing vows.

He knew he would be tempted to slide back into his old ways, and he learned how to resist regression.

But despite Darren's progress, Jennifer—plodding through her own treacherous valley of shadows and groping for the light—could not accept his new reality. She spoke harshly to him, making it apparent that she didn't consider him worthy of her forgiveness.

Darren made another vow: to prove to her that he had changed. Over the next few months, Jennifer witnessed Darren's spiritual growth while she sought her own restoration in God. Her heart eventually softened, and the positive changes he saw in her made him more determined to succeed than ever.

One day Darren received a letter from Jennifer.[2] It said,

> Dear Darren:
>
> I wanted to say thank you for that night when you reached out to me and I pulled away. It was a hard night for me. It was painful, yet healing at the same time. I've had to remind myself it was okay—you are not the one who hurt me so long ago. But you look so much like him! For a split second, I wanted you to say, "I'm sorry I hurt you." I wanted you to say, "I'll stop the madness now and give back your soul I took so long ago." I wanted you to say, "It was wrong . . . I will stop hurting you now." Then I realized you could not do that; you are not him.
>
> With your continued care and comfort, healing began to stir within me.
>
> Once you were a sex offender, but you've changed. Now you are a man who cares and knows pain . . . not my pain, but your own.
>
> I don't really know what I'm trying to say. Maybe this note is stupid. I just want you to know that I was okay with you tonight, and that I see a good man inside. I never thought I would see or say that about you, or anyone else in

the abuse recovery group. I guess that's what healing is all about. I guess that's what this group is all about.

Now I want to say thank you. Thank you for helping me find a piece of healing.

Jennifer

Jennifer learned she could make a choice to heal, or she could choose to stay sick in her hatred for her perpetrators. In order to survive her future, she knew what she had to do. Her choice to heal was not easy. She didn't even know if she wanted to change—but the pain was almost unbearable. She had to learn to let go of fear, to trust, and forgive others—the hardest challenge of all.

Eventually, by the grace of God, forgiveness came and she was finally free. It's only by God's power that we are able to accomplish anything, especially what we believe to be unattainable.

I felt incredible compassion as I began to see perpetrators through the eyes of God. Forgiveness crept into my heart. The meetings ended with prayer, and it felt eerie to hold the hand of a rapist without feeling rage.

I started viewing rapists as fellow human beings made in the image of God. I felt free of my clouded perception. I wanted others to find the same freedom from the strongholds of their wounds. I wanted to help them. I enrolled in an intensive two-year lay counseling program at Good Samaritan Ministries, and stayed an additional two years as a volunteer counselor.

once upon a Horse

She spoke to me in the aloneness of my silent
world, bright star of my life,
her copper coat gleaming in the sun,
her muzzle smelling sweet.
Take me away on phantom journeys,
flying over green fields and swollen streams,
damp velvet blanket of rippling muscles
soft beneath my skin.
The rhythm of her hoofbeats rings music in my
ears. Her tail flies high, bringing
me safely home again.
Pushing her head into my face, nickering softly,
begging for oats, she gazes at me with dark liquid eyes.
Oh to feel the magic one more time of
riding the wind upon my horse . . .
once upon my horse again.

—Leila

chapter 8

God can create New Life

One night after an abuse recovery meeting, a lady came to me and told me that her husband traveled a lot. "I'm afraid the same thing will happen to me that happened to you," she said. "I'm afraid someone will break into my home."

"I can't guarantee that won't happen," I said, "and I understand why you're fearful—but you don't have to be bound by fear."

I told her to claim Psalm 4:8, "I will lie down and sleep in peace, for you alone, O LORD, make me dwell in safety," and to put the Scripture under her pillow.

Another friend told me, "The man who raped me is due to be released from prison soon. I'm afraid he might try to find me."

We prayed together, and then I told her, too, that she didn't have to be bound by fear. Psalm 18:2 says, "The LORD is my rock, my fortress and my deliverer; my God is my rock, in whom I take refuge. He is my shield and the horn of my salvation, my stronghold."

I offered these women more, of course, than prayer and Scripture. The abuse recovery meetings are all about support and healing. I know that memories of pain linger in the depths of their souls, and their scars will not completely disappear. The point I wanted to make to these women is that I can't eliminate the *cause* of their fear, but they don't have to let fear control their lives.

The truth is, I couldn't promise them that they'd never be

assaulted. I couldn't promise them that they'd never be assaulted *again*. I could only pray to God that they wouldn't be.

The kind of fear these two women experienced had to do with the future. I know that kind of fear. The future is unpredictable, it scares me, too. Fear is the most crippling affliction. But I don't have to be bound by fear because I can trust God for the future . . . He's already there.

I've already talked about the difference between fear and worry (p. 43), and in part 2, I talk more about dealing with fear (chapter 10). But here and now, I give you this: God can help you deal with fear. Bruce Larson, in his book *Living Beyond Our Fears*, says, "Fear is the handle by which we lay hold on God. The opposite of fear is faith. When you stop running and face your fear head on with faith, you find God. It is His presence and power that move us beyond our fears—past, present and future."[1] That's why I offer the women in my group prayer and Scripture—they help us face our fears.

While I pray that God will keep us all safe, the other side of the coin is that adversity strengthens us. A life without trials leaves our muscles too weak to deal with troubles. But when we've been tried and have survived, we build emotional and spiritual strength, and that gives us confidence that we can bear up under other crises that may come our way.

The pain and devastation that come with any trial can guide us, too, toward maturity and inner healing. The insights I've learned about myself and about the human instinct for survival are invaluable when supporting other women who have been traumatized. No one, of course, wants bad things to happen in order to reap a positive outcome, but I know good *will* eventually prevail even if right now we see no possibilities. Luis Palau said,

> There will always come a time (or more likely, times) when tragic events invade our lives, bearing no trace of God's

purposes and no hint of rational explanation. What do we do in those times? The only thing we can do. We trust in the character of a loving God, a righteous God, a holy and compassionate God, who always does right. We will not always understand His ways, but can always trust His character. That is the ultimate conviction that must sustain all of us, even when the answers we seek to life's tragedies escape our most searching gaze.[2]

As I said in a previous chapter, attitudes are the result of how we perceive reality, and fear of the future can dramatically affect our perception of life now. That's why perception is a key factor in recovery. Generally, it isn't the trauma itself that sends us into a tailspin, but our perception of it. If we perceive the trauma as evidence that God doesn't love us, or that life is out to get us, or as punishment for some wrongdoing, those attitudes become our personal agenda, and other realities in life are perceived as fulfilling that agenda.

Allowing God not only to unbind me from fear but also to enlighten my perception softened my heart, making it easier to forgive. Part 2 of this book tells you how I learned to deal with my intrusive, negative thoughts of the past. I learned to dismiss them with positive ones . . . most of the time. I learned to forgive those who had wronged me, and *not* forget the person I had been, lest I return to being that angry, bitter woman. I began to renew my faith daily so the Evil One (Satan) wouldn't test me in a weak moment and try to destroy my newfound freedom.

I haven't yet "arrived," however. While I still don't trust *everyone*, that doesn't mean I don't trust *anyone*. It's not paranoia to be suspicious of some people, and relying on my intuition is using wisdom.

As I move farther and farther away from my past, my memory dims: dates and events blur together, making me wonder if it all really happened. Then out of nowhere, something occurs to awaken memories inside my head: a dream, an event, something someone did or said—a scene from a movie. And once again the long lost past springs to life. But when that happens, I can steady myself, remember how far I've come, and keep going.

For most of us, recovery is a gradual process. It moves silently, unsuspected, drawing us closer to peace with each advancing year. One morning a few years ago, I stumbled into a men's Bible study my husband was hosting. When the visitors asked how I was, I replied, "Fine, except for my nightmares." I was immediately surrounded. They laid hands on me and asked God to free my mind from those night terrors. After they prayed, I said, "Thanks, guys," and went about my day. A few weeks later, I realized that since that prayer was prayed over me, I'd had only a couple of mild nightmares.

Believe me, I understand why rape survivors want to hurry and heal. They often ask me, "What's the plan? Do you have a twelve-step program? I want to get started right away and be recovered by next Christmas." But recovery doesn't work that way. Recovery comes from maturing in our thinking, a turnaround in our perception. We must cease blaming others for our bad attitudes and forgive those who have inflicted pain in our lives. Recovery comes to us in the light of education, learning, and understanding evil.

Satan and his fallen angels are evil, and their mission is to destroy humankind, especially by infiltrating our thoughts and minds. This is why the world is a mess and people commit evil acts. Discernment of evil doesn't dissolve the impact of our traumas, but remember, just because *one* man sexually assaulted you (or even if there was more than one) doesn't mean *all* men are evil. We can let evil acts destroy us, or we can, with God's help, triumph over them.

So don't let your heart become hardened. If it has already, ask God to give you a new heart—one free of hate and bitterness. With a new heart comes new life. Remember the visiting pastor's prophecy about celebrating something special in six months' time (p. 42).

The prophecy came to pass. A move back to the Portland area found my husband and me observing a joyful Christmas reunion with our family—exactly six months from the date of the prophecy!

What's remarkable about that celebration is merely the joy of it. I'd been taking antidepressants for six years and had decided no longer to let a pill control my happiness. I needed to be responsible for my own emotions, at least in part. During the six years I took antidepressants, they gave me the ability to see life with clarity. I was able to process my thoughts in an orderly fashion. Panic attacks, anxiety, and depression ceased. However, my hair fell out, I gained weight, and with one medication, I passed out.

It was time to quit taking them. Stopping wasn't easy . . . I struggled. The longer I went without medication, however, the less I was depressed. Depression still knocks at my door occasionally, but I don't reach for a pill, I reach for God. I pray—even if I don't feel like it. I know it sounds too simple, but try it. It worked for me, and it just might work for you, too.

I'm not suggesting for everyone to go off antidepressants. (Always check with your doctor before going off medication. Some medications should not be stopped abruptly.) They are vital for some people, making the difference between life and death. For those who want to quit taking antidepressants, however, there are other ways to help manage depression: support groups, cognitive therapy, and the power of Jesus Christ! Invite Him into your heart. He is your comforter and healer. In His own time He will make everything come together for good—He has for me.

My rape carried me away to the pit of hell, and I never dreamed that, like the phoenix, I would rise up to a life of wholeness. I've forgiven my perpetrator, and I no longer look at men with disdain. I'm free from the strongholds of pain that bound me to the past. And now, I can quit blaming myself for allowing that pain to turn me into someone not very likable.

Time does not heal all wounds of the heart. Only the power of

God's Son can do that. But our sorrows need not be a waste. We are to use the pain that comes into our lives to help others overcome their pain. As you seek and trust God, your purpose will most likely be revealed.

If you desire freedom from the strongholds of your pain (past or present), you can recover from your wounding with God's help. You can be free from the power of darkness that binds you to the past. Ask God for wings to fly away from the snares that keep you grounded. Ask Him to give you the promise He gave me: *I will bring peace to your life like the calm on the morning pond.* Invite Him to journey with you. Trust Him. You won't be sorry.

Part 2

RESTRUCTURING YOUR LIFE AFTER SEXUAL ASSAULT

Dear Reader

Recovery from your sexual assault will find its own pace. Perhaps your wounds are ancient, but you've never fully recovered, and you're now ready for the process of healing. Or perhaps your wound is as fresh now as yesterday. Just reading and listening to things on the subject of rape may be challenging for you. That's okay. This book is meant to be used as a tool in your recovery, either alone or in a class setting. It is only a means to an end. (If you are suicidal, out of control, or feel you're still in a post-traumatic stress, high-risk situation, seek professional help *immediately*. You don't want to retraumatize yourself. Revisiting trauma with your therapist/ doctor is a safe place for you.)

Rape is rape, whether it is committed by your father, uncle, brother, neighbor, or a stranger. While this book primarily addresses rape, the material is beneficial to survivors of any type of sexual abuse (incest, molestation, etc.).

The purpose for women sharing their thoughts in a group setting is so they can learn as a team how to be free of anger, bitterness, fear, and sorrow. If you are studying alone, God is on the journey to wholeness with you.

In any event, survivors of sexual assault walk the same path. You've been damaged. Your world has changed. But whether you get better or worse is up to you. Evil can be destroyed, its wreckage left behind, and God can create new life in you. In a group, others can take part in the birthing of your new life.

If you're reading the book by yourself, please work through the questions following each chapter, writing down your answers. Doing that is a powerful tool and will play a significant role in your recovery. Find a trusted friend or relative to share your writing with, who will be your confidante, encouraging you on.

If you continue turning these pages, I salute you—you are a woman of courage!

For those who want to help rape survivors recover, I salute you, too. It takes as much courage to help others as it does for those who seek help.

Participants in a rape recovery group should agree to the following:

- I will attend all meetings, be on time, and contact the group leader if unable to meet these requirements.
- I will let the leader know if I am unable to finish the class.
- I understand that first names only are to be used.
- I will respect the person speaking by giving my full attention.
- I will not bring children or unauthorized visitors to a meeting.
- I will not make audio or video recordings during any part of the meeting.
- I will not disclose information about a group member to outsiders.
- I will not abuse substances on the day of the meeting.
- I understand that the leader has the authority to remove any participant from the group if deemed necessary in order to maintain the integrity of the group.

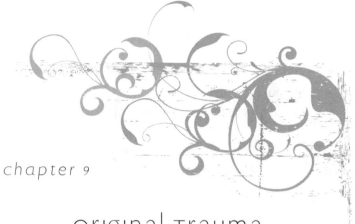

original trauma

Man is the only animal who causes pain to others
with no other object than wanting to do so.

—Arthur Schopenhauer

Rape causes a crisis in a woman's life. It makes her feel over-whelmed, powerless, and out of control. All the familiar ways of managing and dealing with the world don't seem to work anymore.

Rape is likely the worst trauma a woman would ever have to face in her life. All components of a woman's self are violated in a sexual assault. Her property rights are trespassed—perhaps her home or car was entered illegally. Her personal possessions are plundered or used as weapons to tie, gag, blindfold, or hurt her. Her physical being is threatened, handled without consent, and usually injured. The most appalling of invasions occurs, that of her inner self. There is no greater insult that can be committed by one human being against another.[1]

Victimization, which means the process of becoming a victim, can occur on three levels:[2]

- Level One: the original trauma (such as sexual assault)

- Level Two: the secondary wounding (such as your loved ones not believing you)
- Level Three: the response of society to the trauma

I'll discuss these three levels in the following chapters. Let's begin here, though, by examining the survivor's reactions to the original trauma.

shock

You've experienced trauma, and you are (or were) in shock as a result. Your system went into overload in order to deal with your new reality. This happens to everyone encountering trauma, especially rape.

Our bodies and minds make up the whole of our being. When trauma hits you, your body and mind are rattled as if in an earthquake, making you temporarily disjointed. Shock is the immediate aftermath that leaves you emotionally and physically numb, confused, and in a state of hyper arousal.

Hyper arousal occurs because, when the trauma hit, your senses went on full alert. Oddly, well after the trauma is over, they remain on full alert. The switch that was turned on doesn't turn off, maintaining a state of hyper arousal. The effects are trouble sleeping, difficulty concentrating, heightened vigilance, being easily startled, feeling wary, sudden crying, unexpected anger, deeper emotions, panicking, intensified alertness, increased anxiety, and reminders of the trauma. This leads to physical reactions such as a rapid heartbeat and sweating.[3]

The effects of shock can cause you to question the memory of your trauma, thereby minimizing it: "Maybe it wasn't as bad as I thought." After a trauma such as rape, you tend to think differently. Your memory, emotions, and perceptions are not the same as before.

Denial and Disbelief

These reactions typically occur after the initial impact of the trauma. *Denial* is refusing to believe that something exists. Denial can be your friend immediately after a trauma. Temporary denial, in small doses, protects you and allows you to cope with feelings of helplessness, abandonment, the fear of the perpetrator returning, and the fear of death.

When the shock of emotional wounding has occurred, denial is necessary. The overwhelming impact of rape needs the softening, anesthetic balm of denial. Denial distracts your mind so that you can recover at your own pace. Your trauma tells your mind to refuse the reality of your rape as being too painful to face.

Although you may not be aware of it, God carries you in the palm of His hand during this time. The psalmist writes, "For in the time of trouble he shall hide me in his pavilion" (27:5 KJV). Shock and denial will pass in time. You can then accept what occurred and move forward.

Disbelief is, by far, the overriding effect on your thinking. While denial is the *refusal* to believe, disbelief a state in which you *cannot* believe what has happened to you. Like denial, disbelief is protective. It keeps you from processing your thoughts and experience as reality, which are, at the moment, incomprehensible.

There is no preparation for shocking and sudden events. Because you couldn't prepare for rape, there is not a place in your cognition for it. A place has to be created in your thoughts *after* the trauma.[4]

Rage and Anger

Rage and anger are normal reactions following rape: anger at the rapist, anger that the assault took place, anger at the disruption of your life, anger at those close to you, and anger that life seems to go on happily for everyone else while your life has been torn apart. The slightest thing can cause anger to erupt. You may wonder where your abrupt anger comes from. It might even scare you because you suddenly feel out of control.

In time, this abrupt rage and anger will cease. Be patient. And remember, these episodes of rage won't last forever. Seek counseling if your anger and rage continues.

Guilt

Many rape victims second-guess themselves, wondering if they did something to entice the rapist. Some victims may harbor the thought that their rape is punishment for some past sin. These responses, while common, are nonetheless totally without foundation. The crime of rape has everything to do with the mind of the rapist and nothing to do with the victim.

Depression

When a person has been subjected to severe stress, such as rape, the biological neurotransmitter system is disturbed. This system becomes so strained it cannot perform its functions as it did before the traumatic event. This physiological breakdown can lead to negative thinking, lack of concentration, low self-esteem, hopelessness, difficulty in decision making, and sleep disorders. Other classic symptoms of depression are irritability, anxiety, loss of pleasure in others and in activities, and a heightened sensitivity to the reactions of others.

Depression often grabs hold of a traumatized person, yet it doesn't always happen immediately. It can surface much later, after the trauma has occurred. With so many issues to address after sexual assault, depression is often camouflaged. When you're left with the feeling of loss (losing your old self, loss of a reliable world, loss of safety, etc.), depression can take over. Depression can also affect attitudes or memories of past losses, compounding this out-of-control condition.

Depression can leave you feeling fatigued, powerless, helpless, sad, lethargic, down on yourself, uninterested in life, or suicidal. Depression usually passes, however, when your normal way of living has been resumed, your mourning is completed, and you start taking steps to resolution, such as rape recovery classes or counseling.

If you think your suffering from depression and if it persists, see your doctor for a physical exam and find out if antidepressants might help you. Extended counseling may also be beneficial.

Bargaining

Sometimes a rape survivor tries to bargain with God: "If you make the pain go away, I'll never commit that recurring sin of mine again." This kind of bargaining adds to the survivor's feelings of guilt, and that is unhealthy thinking.

*   *   *

While rape is frightening, disgusting, and painful, it is not the end of the world. You are the same worthwhile, lovely person you were before. You don't have to be marked a victim for life. The following chapters will help you choose your own response, which will allow you to stay in control and never be destroyed.

QUESTIONS TO ANSWER

1. Name your anger. Identify one or more persons you are angry at right now.
2. What kind of denying or bargaining, if any, have you made?
3. Describe your original trauma. Where were you raped? Was your rapist a stranger or an acquaintance?

chapter 10

Fear and the Loss of safety

We crucify ourselves between two thieves: regret for yesterday and fear for tomorrow.

—Fulton Oursler

The most widespread fear experienced by rape survivors is the fear of death. In surveys conducted, over half of all survivors did not expect to live through the rape. Rape is, after all, a crime of violence and aggression, not a crime of passion. For rapists, sex is a weapon used to degrade women and cause them pain. So during a rape, the woman fears for her life.

Studies have found that if you were raped in a "safe" place, such as your home, post-traumatic stress will be greater than if the assault occurred in a place you considered dangerous, such as an isolated street late at night. More women are raped in their own homes, in fact, than in any other place.[1]

Rape victims are left fearful in their homes and communities. They are left with anxiety, nightmares, insomnia, addiction to tranquilizers, health problems, and fatigue.

Nancy Vanable Raine, in her book *After Silence*, writes,

The loss of the sense of safety is impossible to regain once you have lost it. The sense of safety is not like other senses . . . smell, taste, sight. It has no companions that can compensate for its absence. It stands alone, beneath, like the foundation below ground that supports a building. When the sense of safety and bodily autonomy have been destroyed, all that it supports crumbles. Its loss changes the relation between self and the world.

. . . The need to feel safe can become an addiction that cannot be satisfied by external measures, although it takes many years to discover this. There will never be enough locks, security cameras, dogs, or doormen to satisfy this craving. When the sense of safety is destroyed, the temptation to construct it outside the self is itself the source of more addictions. You can spend a fortune and still find yourself sitting alone in the dark, trembling. Precautions, no matter how elaborate and sound, remain on the surface, like Sargasso. No roots descend into the mysterious depths where the wreck truly lies.[2]

Traumatic events are things that happen outside usual experiences—events that are so intensely frightening, painful, and threatening that they overwhelm your ability to feel secure about the world. If you continue to feel overwhelmed by the trauma of rape, the process of healing includes learning to become aware of, and be honest about, the fear that so strongly damaged your sense of security.[3]

The human nervous system, which includes the brain and all the various networks of nerves, is our central computer system for processing information about what is happening inside and outside the body. This computer sends commands to the rest of the body, telling all the parts how to act in response to the information it has gathered about current conditions.

One particular type of command of the nervous system occurs whenever we perceive the conditions around us to be sufficiently threatening. This command is known as the "fight or flight" reflex. It switches on autopilot when certain conditions tell us that threat is nearby, that is, when we are frightened. When this command is given, a series of electrochemical events takes place within our bodies that affect heart rate, breathing, muscle tension levels, various chemical fluid balances, and a lot more. The "fight or flight" reflex alerts our bodies quickly and helps us survive the danger. However, this reflex cannot distinguish between real and imaginary danger. Every time we believe there is something threatening us—even if we are interpreting the situation incorrectly—the "fight or flight" reflex produces a jolt of energy.[4]

Fear resulting from rape is true fear. It is equivalent to seeing a train racing toward you, or knowing your plane is about to go down, or having someone try to break into your home. Unfounded fear, though, is also crippling. Worry, which is unfounded fear, is not true fear. Worry is anticipating that something awful is going to happen. If, for example, I'm worried that the elevator will get stuck, the ship will go down, or the horse will fall, I'll refuse to enter an elevator, go on a cruise, or ride a horse.

When something appears threatening, a trauma survivor sees not only what's going on in the present, but also remembers previous trauma. The line between what is real and what is not becomes blurred. To distinguish between real and unfounded fear, ask yourself, "Is this situation a question of my survival?" If your answer is *no*, your "fight or flight" reflex intensity will be reduced, and your pounding heart will calm down.

It isn't so much that you fear another assault. It's the unpredictable future that scares you. As I noted earlier (p. 76), fear is the most crippling affliction known to humankind, and it can be the driving force in your perception of life. If you have been raped, it's normal to be fearful. And while you cannot eliminate the causes of fear, you don't have to let fear control your life. Do whatever it takes to feel safe. You may want to stay a short time with a friend or family member.

Eventually, those scary feelings will pass. But remember that everyone recovers at a different pace. It may take weeks, months, or years. If fear and pain linger too long, however, don't hesitate to seek professional counseling to resolve it. And above all, trust God for the future—He's already there.

safety and Assertiveness

The healing process begins by feeling safe. You can begin to feel safe by changing your environment and by changing your thoughts and behaviors. How you'll establish a sense of safety depends on the nature of your trauma. You're the only one who knows what will make you feel safe.

Empowerment begins by taking care of yourself physically and emotionally. Your traumatic experience left you feeling helpless in the face of danger. Feeling safe and secure is now your prime goal. Feeling safe will leave you comfortable with your emotions.

Establishing safety for your home might include improved locks for doors and windows, securing basement windows, removing overgrown shrubs near windows and doors, installing a security system, having a cell phone by your bed, or even adopting a dog. At night, leave a couple of lights on inside, and leave porch lights on or install motion sensing lights that come on automatically.

Other safety precautions may include carrying a cell phone, parking as close to buildings as possible, and asking a fellow employee to walk you to your car after work when it is dark.

Always maintain your car in good running order, avoid parking in dark, out-of-the-way places, and make sure your car always has at least a half tank of gas. Carry a HELP! CALL POLICE! banner in your car. Take a self-defense class.

Assertiveness Training Exercise

This exercise has proven helpful to trauma survivors. It will immediately help you feel more empowered.

If you're studying this book as a group, divide the group in half, with each person facing another. The object is to walk toward each other, one pair at a time, and pass each other, walking tall, shoulders back, head held erect, with relaxed, loose hands.

This exercise is especially important to rape survivors. It will give you a sense of confidence and control. Your assertive posture tells others, "Don't get any silly ideas—you may get more than you bargained for!"

Do this with a friend if you aren't in a group setting.

QUESTIONS TO ANSWER

1. What was your greatest fear during the rape? Were children or loved ones present at the time? Did the perpetrator make threats? Did he act erratically, adding more danger to your assault?

2. What is your greatest fear now? If the criminal got away, do you fear his return? If he is soon to be released from prison, do you fear he might try to find you and retaliate?

3. Name additional safety precautions you can take.

4. If you performed the assertiveness training exercise, how did you feel before, during, and after the exercise?

chapter 11

Post-Traumatic stress

Post-Traumatic Stress has been called a sane reaction to an insane situation.

—Benjamin Colodzin

Everyone faces a crisis sometime during life. The crisis can be as small as losing your car keys, to as severe as losing a loved one. These crises are stressful, but not traumatic. Traumatic events refer to situations in which great danger is involved. In these cases, you are powerless and helpless, and the trauma horrific. These are not normal, everyday events.

The magnitude of such events overtaxes your ability to cope. Everyone confronts the fact of mortality, but for a rape survivor the reality of death has been confronted more vividly than for most people.

Benjamin Colodzin, Ph.D., says in *How to Survive Trauma*, "I do not like to use the term 'Post-Traumatic Stress Disorder' since it is not always useful to think of this pattern of functioning as a medical disorder. Therefore, I will drop the D for disorder." He goes on to say, "It makes it easier to concentrate on the person who has lived through something overwhelming rather than on symptoms of a disease. So, we will refer to PTSD as Post-Traumatic Stress."[1]

Your experience of rape has changed the color of your world

forever. Once any trauma, in fact, has occurred, the illusion that the world is safe is destroyed. Gone forever.[2]

Some symptoms of traumatic stress have been covered earlier, such as rage/anger, depression, shock, denial, and disbelief. Now we'll add some new ones to the list:

- Hyper-alert response: constant vigilance and scanning, always looking around as though something dangerous is about to happen
- Hyper-startle response: being jumpy, edgy, easily startled
- Memory and concentration interrupted: memory recall short and concentration difficult
- Anxiety: physical tension, leading to stomachaches, headaches, back pain, and the mind carrying worry of unfounded fears, terror, and fear of death
- Panic: feeling like you're coming apart inside, associated with the fear that you will be harmed (raped) again; feeling out of control and unable to cope. Being alone, remembering your brush with death, knowing this is an unsafe world, and hearing, seeing, or smelling something that reminds you of the event, can bring on a panic attack
- Mood swings: can happen any time, any day. You can feel great one minute, then awful the next
- Psychic numbing: an inability to experience love, playfulness, joy, or bonding with other people

When traumatic crises hit, you may be overwhelmed by a state of emotional instability, a sort of temporary insanity characterized by intense fear and often painful physical symptoms. The usual coping mechanisms are inadequate. New ways of dealing with this period of dangerous stress must be found. Your perceptions of reality become totally distorted, and your life becomes a whirlwind of confusion, fear, and depression.[3]

If you learn new problem-solving techniques—face the crises head-on—and resolve any issues that arise, you will grow. If, however, you let your grief and pain bury you, you will drown in your suffering and ultimately regress into an emotional basket case. You are under the crushing weight of severe emotional pain and deep psychological wounds. The wounds are prone to reopening time and time again.[4]

QUESTIONS TO ANSWER

1. Can you name other side effects of rape?
2. What were your symptoms of post-traumatic stress? Do you still experience them?

chapter 12

Depression

Mental illness, like the falling leaves . . . the quiet death no one sees.

—Janet Valenta Allen

There's a difference between feeling depressed and having clinical depression. We all feel depressed from time to time for one reason or another—a rainy day, the dog died, the house needs numerous repairs. Clinical depression, however, is physiological, a medical condition brought on by changes of the biochemistry in the brain, and/or alterations in hormonal secretions.

Emotional jolts and sudden shocks, as well as long-term stress, may alter the balance of brain chemicals and/or hormone production. Sudden trauma, as rape, may affect the neurotransmitter system, which produces the chemical messengers of the brain. If necessary treatment is not taken, the balance can get further out of kilter. This alteration can be temporary or long lasting, and often remains out of balance, a condition thought to play a role in clinical depression. When under severe and prolonged stress, as one might undergo after a rape—harassment, trials, changes in personal relationships—the body produces an excess of the hormone cortisol, which is thought also to play a role in clinical depression.

Under these biochemical and hormonal alterations, the brain cannot perform its functions as it did before the traumatic event. This inability is known as clinical depression. Some symptoms of clinical depression are hypersensitivity to others, irritability, anxiety, loss of the ability to experience peace, sleep disturbances, and a general loss of interest in life.

In his book *The Surprising Truth About Depression*, Dr. Herbert Wagemaker declared, "Depression is difficult to describe. You might say depression is just a feeling. You might say it's like living inside a dark cloud—no light, no hope. Then again, you might liken depression to a state of paralysis. You can't think. You can't even move. You feel like you simply can't go on with your life. These kinds of feelings are incomprehensible to those who have never suffered from depression. But to those who have, they are woven into the very fabric of their lives."[1]

suicidal Thoughts

Suicidal thoughts are brought on by intense feelings of despair and hopelessness. To some sexual assault survivors, living is viewed as more painful than dying. If you are plagued by suicidal thoughts, depression may be the culprit. Seek a psychiatrist for counseling and perhaps an antidepressant. Wagemaker writes, "Some Christians sometimes have suicidal thoughts. When you are in the midst of depression, you don't have control of such thoughts. This is also a part of depression, especially severe depression. What you do have control over is whether or not you seek out treatment, and you should do so as soon as possible."[2]

If you are struck by sudden and overwhelming thoughts of suicide, grasp onto this thought: You survived your assault; you will survive your recovery. Every city has suicide-prevention centers and twenty-four-hour hotlines, and you can always call 911. Your life is worth a phone call. Seek help.

Another way to defeat suicidal thoughts is to sign a suicide contract with your counselor, a trusted friend, or family member. The contract states that you won't harm yourself—that you will call one of them if you're feeling out of control.

Balancing Exercise

Your life needs balance in order for you to move past your trauma and function in your daily tasks. By "balanced," I mean to have your physical, mental, and spiritual feet planted in such a way that whatever happens in your life cannot easily knock you off kilter. One of the best ways to learn about balance is by practicing it.[3]

Many cultures have their own variations of an exercise called Pushing Hands. I learned about this exercise in a mental health class in college, and then discovered it again in the book *How to Survive Trauma* by Benjamin Colodzin.

It goes like this: Two people stand and face each other, two or three feet apart, legs slightly spread, toes pointed forward. Place your arms in front of you, palms forward and fingers raised, lined up with the other player's hands. You may lean forward on your toes or backward on your heels, but you may not move your foot position. If you move your foot position, this is defined as losing your balance—and the game.

You may make contact only with the hands of the other player. You may push as hard as you want. The object is not to make yourself the victor and the other person the loser, but simply to avoid losing your balance. Balance is using an efficient amount of energy to achieve your goals; winning is defined as the ability to push outward with your force and to receive the force of the other player without either of you moving your foot position.[4]

You can easily lose your physical balance because of mental or emotional imbalances that come up while you are engaged in playing the game. This game makes you aware that it's sometimes necessary to bend in order to maintain your balance. Pushing Hands begins to make you aware of your own particular style of projecting and receiving force, and provides opportunities to learn how to handle force in a balanced manner. For example, force is "excessive" when its use causes you or the other person to lose your balance.

Does the slightest provocation cause you to lose your balance like a top-heavy vase knocked over with the slightest bump? Maybe you've taken on too much and need to say no to new tasks. Pushing Hands teaches us that we must learn to bend without breaking when unexpected pressures push against us.[5]

QUESTIONS TO ANSWER

1. Are you consumed with depression or suicidal thoughts? If so, are you seeking treatment?
2. What are you doing to find balance in your life?

shame and guilt

Do not let me be put to shame, nor let my enemies triumph over me.

—Psalm 25:2

My guilt has overwhelmed me like a burden too heavy to bear.

—Psalm 38:4

After rape, women experience a sense of shame and guilt.

shame

Shame: A painful mental feeling aroused by a sense of having done something wrong or dishonorable or improper or ridiculous.[1]

Many rape survivors and their families are bound by shame. They worry over what others will think; they feel ashamed if they are not believed; they fear exposing themselves to the reactions of others. Shame is what prevents a survivor from talking about the experience. Shame attacks the survivor by making her think she's a bad person. Shame is that feeling that no one wants to be left alone with you for fear you might speak of your assault, or remind them of their own vulnerability. Shame can be more debilitating than guilt.

Shame, however, is what the rapist, not the victim, should feel. Yet the victim takes on the perpetrator's shame, rendering her mute. Shame makes her feel being a *victim of rape* is a crime.

According to Michael Lewis, in his study *Shame: The Exposed Self*, an intense feeling of shame can cause memory loss. Shame silences because it encloses the entire self. Rape shame is hard to escape.[2]

Willard Gaylin writes, "Aristotle describes shame as the feeling that involves things that are disgraceful to ourselves or to those we care for. Shame is fear of a public exhibition of wrongdoing, of being exposed in front of the group. He recognized this when he said, 'Shame is a mental picture of disgrace in which we shrink from the disgrace itself, and not from its consequences.'"[3]

Others besides the victim experience shame. Mothers are reluctant to tell their husbands of their daughters' rapes. One woman said, "My husband suffers from depression. I just don't think he can handle the news. It will traumatize him." This was a husband that handled everything else without falling apart. He held a job, had hobbies, and was active in church. Was she afraid her husband would be ashamed of his daughter? She didn't want to find out.

Another woman said to her daughter, "Don't tell your father!"

Yet another woman wouldn't tell *her* mother (the grandmother) about her daughter's rape. She said, "My mother wouldn't understand." What was there to understand? The granddaughter was raped. The grandmother was a strong Christian. Had she known, it's likely she would have been supportive of her daughter and granddaughter and held them up in prayer.

Perhaps the mothers were secretly judging their daughter's actions prior to the rape. Were these mothers ashamed? Is that why they kept silent? Secrets are harmful—harmful to the one keeping it, to the one from whom it is withheld, and most of all to the victim, making her feel ashamed for something over which she had no control.

Lewis Smedes writes in his book, *Shame and Grace*, "People invent many ways to escape their shame. None of them work. They only push the shame out of the front door of their feelings and let it in again through the back door. The better way to deal with shame is not to escape it but to heal it."[4]

To help combat shame and guilt, keep a log and write down when you have these feelings. For example, "I feel ashamed because I shared about my rape with a friend I hadn't seen in a long time. She was visibly embarrassed." Write in your log why you shouldn't be ashamed: "I'm not ashamed. Mary is the one with the problem over hearing of my assault."

When shame tries to overtake you, talk to a trusted friend. Hearing yourself talk aloud helps make sense of your feelings, and you need to hear affirmative words from others.

You can be healed of unwarranted shame! You can be healed of your fermenting resentment toward those who have made you feel ashamed. Part of that healing is to forgive the one who has shamed you. You can do this only with the gift of God's grace, so ask Him to give you grace for forgiveness and to remove your unwarranted feelings of shame and unworthiness.

Guilt

Guilt is feeling you are at blame for something.[5] Feelings of guilt can be overwhelming and can suffocate your happiness and take over your life. Many rape survivors suffer from feelings of guilt, believing they have done something wrong when they haven't, thinking, for example, *I wore a sexy dress; therefore, the rape is my fault.* Guilt feelings can lead to thoughts of unworthiness that creep in and permeate your days and your emotions. Obsessive thoughts take over until you truly believe you are a bad person. It's odd that the victim should experience feelings of guilt when the rapist is the one who bears *true* guilt.

One pretty brunette, a homeschooled seventeen-year-old girl, was brought to me by her parents for counseling. She had gone on a foreign mission trip, and while there she was gang raped by several men. She didn't tell anyone at the time. When I asked her why she didn't, she answered, "I was told when arriving, the guards were supposed to protect us. If they didn't, they would be shot and killed. I didn't want them to die." Never mind the most vicious, cruel act was committed upon an innocent young woman. She stuffed her pain so they wouldn't be killed, thus relieving her of any guilt.

The sadness of this story is threefold. One: the horror of her rape; two: anger that her parents never prepared her for evil—neither did the church; three: a secondary wounding when her pastor told her that maybe God allowed the rape to break her spirit of pride. After that scolding, she probably thought, *I'm a bad person. I deserved it!*"

Living with chronic guilt instead of dealing with it can be destructive, having a powerful impact on your mental and physical health. Some outcomes of chronic guilt are depression, anxiety, low self-esteem, the need to be in control, anger, and unforgiveness. Staying focused on guilt—characterized by "If only I had . . ." thinking—rather than moving toward resolution hinders your well-being and recovery.

When you have been raped, your perspective can be distorted, and your mind can play tricks on you. You can lose the ability to judge between *true* guilt and *feelings* of guilt. If overwhelming guilt consumes you, refuse to accept it as legitimate. Fight it! Tell yourself, "It wasn't my fault. I'm innocent!" Tell that to yourself over and over when guilt attacks you. This will help confront your inaccurate mind-set.

Remember, Satan is the accuser of false guilt. He is the father of lies, attacking us with condemnation, attempting to convince us of undeserved guilt. "Your enemy the devil prowls around like a roaring lion looking for someone to devour. Resist him, standing firm in the faith" (1 Peter 5:8–9). Give yourself permission not to feel guilty. Let go of guilt feelings—let go, and let God help: "Put on the full armor of God so that you can take your stand against the devil's schemes" (Eph. 6:11).

If your guilt feelings are intense or persistent, seek professional help so that you can return to rest, dear ones, and rest in Him.

QUESTIONS TO ANSWER

1. Who has made you feel ashamed?
2. Who can you talk to, to help make sense of your feelings?
3. Have you forgiven those who have shamed you?
4. If you put yourself in harm's way, have you quit blaming yourself?
5. Have you given your guilt feelings to God?

you don't need to forgive yourself

The years teach us much which the days never knew.
—Ralph Waldo Emerson

Are you a victim who put yourself in harm's way before your rape? Perhaps you got drunk and passed out, or maybe you went home with a stranger? Are you plagued with guilt? Have you said, "I'll never forgive myself?" I have good news—you don't need to forgive yourself!

Why? First, your exercising poor judgment or making an unwise decision does not give the perpetrator license to rape. Plenty of men have gone out with women who drank too much or with women who agreed to go to the men's home, and the vast majority of these men did not turn into rapists. Your lapse in judgment did not turn a man into a rapist, it only gave someone who was already a rapist the opportunity to rape.

Second, no Scripture in the Bible commands you to forgive yourself. One young lady who is a Christian told me she'd put herself in harm's way before her rape and couldn't forgive herself. I asked her why she couldn't. After a long pause, she confessed, "I feel like God allowed me to be raped as punishment for my past sins."

While we do suffer the consequences of our sins, when we are in Christ Jesus we can be confident that God does not punish us for those sins. Therefore, we don't need to pardon ourselves, nor *can* we pardon ourselves, for our past sins. God is the one who forgives. God says in Isaiah 43:25, "I, even I, am the one who wipes out your transgressions for My own sake, and *I will not remember your sins*" (NASB, emphasis added).

God in His love may discipline His children to correct us and direct us toward a life of joy and fruitfulness. But there's no benefit from remembering past sins as a form of self-punishment. A pattern of mentally reliving our sins is, in fact, destructive. Because God has already forgiven us, constant mental retrieval of past sins is a sin in itself. Instead, we are to seek forgiveness from God, or forgiveness from others, but not from ourselves. First John 1:9 says, "If we confess our sins He [God] is faithful and righteous to forgive us our sins and to cleanse us from all unrighteousness" (NASB).

Some women who seek self-forgiveness may have unreal expectations. They may be perfectionists or have low self-esteem, and they are constantly berating themselves over and over for what they may have or *may not* have done. The need to chastise themselves may involve a root issue.

One root problem is *real* guilt. While our conscience is first to convict us with real guilt, this kind of conviction is not bad. A guilty conscience can motivate us to ask forgiveness, learn from our misdeeds, and behave responsibly.

Another kind of guilt is *feelings* of guilt, condemnation produced by Satan. Satan tortures us with "shame on you" thoughts such as, "You're a bad person"; "God is not pleased with you"; "How could you have done that?" When we are absorbed with this kind of condemnation we rob ourselves of a joy-filled life. If you have accepted Christ Jesus as your Savior, then accept His forgiveness for your sins. John says in his first letter to the early Christians, "This then is how we know that we belong to the truth, and how we set our hearts at rest in his presence *whenever our hearts condemn us.* For God is greater than our hearts, and he knows everything" (1 John 3:19–20, emphasis added). Ask God for wisdom and courage to face any root problems you may have. Pray a prayer such as this one:

> Lord, forgive me for trying to do Your job of complete forgiveness. Forgive me for being hard on myself. Forgive me for focusing on past sins. Forgive me for foolishly believing I need to forgive myself. Reveal to me any root problems I may have. Help me to feel Your forgiveness in my heart and rejoice in Your grace. In Jesus' name, Amen.

Still feel like you need to forgive yourself after praying? Those are just guilt feelings. We can't always trust our feelings, though. Instead, trade feelings for faith—faith that God's promises are true.

If you made a wrong choice and messed up, confess it to God, ask for forgiveness, and let go of what you're holding against yourself. When former sins come to mind, channel your thinking to dwell upon God's goodness.

God's supernatural love for you is beyond measure. He never loves you less when you mess up. He never loves you more for your good works. God's outstretched arms are waiting for you to run to Him. Let Him forgive you instead of your trying to do His job. Let Him reveal His plan and dreams to you so you can help others heal and live their dreams too. Let go and let God.

QUESTIONS TO ANSWER

1. Why do you feel the need to forgive yourself?
2. What do you suspect is your root problem?
3. What plan will you take to overcome your need to forgive yourself?

chapter 15

memories

Memories are sometimes the uninvited guests whom we must forgive for intruding.

—Janet Valenta Allen

The subconscious is a shadow world. One component of this world is memory. Every day, memories are stored in our subconscious minds, recorded in our brains like a mental tape that we can't erase. As time passes, we don't even realize they still exist.

During traumatic events, our brains produce noradrenalin and release it into the bloodstream. This hormone causes mental flashbulbs to go off in our brain that capture the horrific trauma like a camera. The resulting memory, stored in the subconscious mind, can surface with potency at any given time.

We cannot control subconscious memories. They are stored deeply but can surface at any time. A single instance of terror can alter the chemistry of the brain. The same neurochemical system that triggers the "fight or flight" response (p. 93) also triggers those traumatic memories with vividness. Psychic pain is the result of traumatic memories that invade our minds, painful events we've repressed or would prefer to forget. Carl Jung called this invasion the shadow at its worst.[1]

The more indelible and horrifying the event, the more indelible the memory. When a woman has been sexually assaulted she is given a life sentence of traumatic memories. And the slightest thing—a certain sound or scent associated with the assault—can trigger an instant visual replay of dreaded memories. The memory may flash across her mind as a fragment rather than a coherent story, nonetheless causing her to reexperience the trauma she wants to forget.

Perhaps the trigger is only vaguely similar to the one associated with the rape, but close enough to alarm us. Still, our thoughts and emotions respond to the trigger, demanding that we react today in the same way we reacted at the time of the attack. This kind of reaction is called post-traumatic stress (PTS), a condition that causes a person to react to routine events as if they were the original traumatic event. Say, for instance, a survivor of sexual abuse catches a whiff of a man's aftershave lotion while she's shopping for groceries, and it's the same aftershave her attacker wore. Her brain chemistry causes her to react with the same feelings she experienced during her attack.

George Johnson, in his book *In the Palaces of Memory*, writes,

> The experience [of reading or conversing] causes physical changes in your brain. In a matter of seconds new circuits are formed, memories that can change forever the way you think about the world. . . . Memory leaves its mark so that we are able to carry around the past inside our heads. Every time you walk away from an encounter, your brain has been altered, sometimes permanently.
>
> The obvious but disturbing truth is that people can impose these changes against your will. Someone can say something—an insult, a humiliation; it lives with you as long as you live. The memory is physically lodged inside you like a shard of glass healed inside a wound. . . . Experience

is transformed into memories. Neuron by neuron, we snap together mental structures, constantly evolving palaces of memory that we carry with us until we die. . . . Even as memories are being laid down, the brain is consolidating and rearranging. . . . Remembering . . . is like being in a trance. . . . Raw experience has been converted into a few set pieces. And it is the set pieces that are remembered.[2]

In my case, a sudden noise, murky shadows, a ringing phone at an unexpected hour, or a knock at the door would push the REPLAY button of my memories, leaving me hostage to daytime nightmares.

coping with Triggers

Post-traumatic stress causes us to respond to certain situations and everyday activities in ways that seem peculiar. As I said above, these strange reactions can be triggered by stimuli associated with the attack, and your brain may have recorded that stimuli before, during, and after your rape. Any stimuli can occur unexpectedly, reminding you of what happened previously. Under certain conditions, noises, smells, sights, thoughts, or feelings that are associated with what happened can act as stimuli.[3]

Recognizing these stimuli will help you understand your reactions, leaving you less troubled by their occurrences. For example, your rapist may have told you to remove your clothes. Long after, you're at the doctor's office for your annual checkup and the nurse says, "Remove your clothes." Those words are stimuli that might trigger a negative reaction.

Feeling safe is a major priority in the life of a rape survivor. Therefore, a trigger situation is threatening because, consciously or unconsciously, you feel powerless and vulnerable to attack. Old memories surface, bringing painful thoughts of anger, fear, and grief. Your reactions can make you feel out of control. You think you're going crazy, and the thought that you are mentally ill is terrifying.

Examples of Stimuli

Stimuli	My Reaction	Traumatic Memory
Someone talks gruffly or scowls	Fear, repulsion	Perpetrator ordered me to remove my clothes
White sleeveless blouses	Anxiety	I wore a white sleeveless blouse the night of the rape
Lights go off at night	Pounding heart, sweating, panic	Electricity was cut the night of the rape

As these stimuli surface, recognize they are just cues—not an impending trauma (rape) about to happen. Your fear will subside, giving you control.

When you know your reactions are linked to the past and have nothing to do with the present, you will better manage these feelings of panic. Differentiating the past from the present will make the present feel safer.

Anniversaries

Anniversary dates can have a significant impact on a rape survivor's behavior and emotional well-being. The anniversary date of the trauma can cause concerns to resurface, but holidays and family celebrations may also serve as stimuli for negative reactions because emotions often run high at those times.

The first anniversary of your rape may prove difficult, bringing up memories that you thought had already been put to rest. Many experience PTS as well, but with each passing year your anxiety will diminish. You might try reclaiming your anniversary date by connecting with someone and creating a new tradition to celebrate. Regardless, every year you'll discover new successes on which to focus. You'll realize how far you've come in recovery, leaving you with renewed hope for the future.

QUESTIONS TO ANSWER

1. What specific sounds, smells, tastes, colors, words, objects, or gestures do you remember before, during, and after your rape?
2. If your sexual assault was decades ago, do you still have reactions to certain stimuli? If so, what are those stimuli?
3. List some ways you can perceive the anniversary of your rape in a positive way.
4. List some ways you can self-talk to calm your psyche.

writing to Heal

Give sorrow words.

—William Shakespeare

Keeping our negative feelings locked up is damaging. We need to process, or release, those emotions, and journaling is a good way to do that. Writing our thoughts and feelings down on paper is an opportunity to be honest and open. Honor yourself by writing about your pain, loss, and grief—then it will become a healing experience.

> Writing is a form of prayer that does something no other form of prayer can do: it makes visible the invisible. We have lots of mental clutter, and underneath that clutter are the images, memories, stories, and thoughts that form our spiritual core. In writing, we get a chance to see the clutter, deal with it, and then draw out these treasures from our core. Writing makes this inner world concrete. Our problems become visible. And when we see them clearly, we can then hand them over to the God who comforts and mends. Writing becomes dialogue with oneself. Writing helps the visionary part of us come to life again.[1]

For journaling, and thereby processing, emotions to be effective, you need to write more than, "Today I felt angry." Write it down as if you were telling the experience to a friend: "I was shopping for groceries today, and I felt almost normal for the first time in weeks. Then I caught a whiff of aftershave from a guy over in bananas. It was the same scent worn by the man who raped me. I felt the blood rush from my face, and I even tried to get a better look at the guy to see if he was the one who raped me. Of course it wasn't, and I felt a little foolish, then I felt angry because . . ." You get the idea.

The process may be difficult at first, but as you keep writing, you're likely to notice that it gets easier to express yourself on paper. It will become easier to be honest with yourself about your emotions, and it will give you insights into the subtle differences in emotions, and what stimuli triggers what emotions. As time passes you'll notice a decrease in the intensity of your emotions and the impact they have on you.

Louise DeSalvo says in her book *Writing as a Way of Healing*, "Writing that describes traumatic or distressing events in detail and how we felt about these events then and feel about them now is the only kind of writing about trauma that clinically has been associated with improved health."[2]

writing to god

If you want healing for your soul, eventually you will have to look at your deepest fears, express your most keenly felt regrets, and describe your losses. But this healing journey is not along a lonely pathway or through a solitary valley. Walking beside you will be the One who dries your tears and warms your heart with a comfort that flows from eternity. You will find safety when you meet the God of all comfort.

"You cannot manufacture God's comfort, for it is free. It is a gift. But while you cannot generate comfort, you can ask for it. You can say yes to it, and you can make space in your heart for it. Jesus spoke of this safety, this peace that abides in the mystery of the brightness of God, when He said, 'Peace I leave with you; my peace I give you. I do not give to you as the world gives' (John 14:27)."[3]

Write a letter to God. Tell Him your hurts, and reflect on God's promises. Here are two examples of letters to God:

> Dear God,
>
> I hurt because of the things I've written about. I hurt because I find that I can't say no when I want to. I can't say how I really feel much of the time. I have depression and anxiety problems. I have trouble handling money and I have problems overeating. I have trouble taking good care of myself. I have trouble setting goals, having fun, and feeling joy.
>
> I need Your help to heal whatever has given all these things such a firm hold on me. Help me, please, to heal. There's a lot I don't remember. A lot I don't know for sure. Some things I'm afraid of. I need Your help!
>
> I thank You for what You've done in my life, for the healing You're doing now. I thank You for Your love and mercy and for salvation.
>
> —Jane[4]

> Dear Heavenly Father God,
>
> I come to You with all that I am, asking for restoration. Only You know the depth of my pain; only You can heal the sorrows of my past. Gather me with tenderness under Your wings. Shed light upon my face so that I might feel the warmth of Your mercies. Let me feel Your presence that I might find new strength. Quiet my soul so I might hear Your still, small voice. Whisper Your eternal message of love. Guide me toward new pathways that lead to joy, healing, and forgiveness. Amen.
>
> —Leila

QUESTIONS TO ANSWER

1. Describe your life right now.
2. On a scale of one to ten—ten being the highest level of healing—where are you in your recovery?
3. What happiness have you experienced this past year?
4. What's bothering you the most right now?
5. Write a letter or poem to God and tell Him about your hurt and pain.

secondary wounding

Only those who have lost reality and lived for years in the Land of Cruel, Inhuman Enlightenment, can truly taste the joy in living and prize the transcendent significance of being a part of humanity.

—Marguerite Schehayae

A secondary wound happens when people say things, intentionally or unintentionally, that deepen the wound in your already wounded soul. Secondary wounding often feels as painful as shooting a bullet into your heart. It can be as deadly as the original traumatic event. Healing from your secondary wounding is every bit as important as healing from your original assault.

Here are some examples of wounding remarks that can heap guilt feelings on survivors:

- "If you'd learned how to use a gun, the assault might not have happened."
- "Why were you there in the first place?"
- "I'm sorry you were raped, but we have to continue our own ministries."

Because of the biological changes that can occur after a rape, victims become exceptionally sensitive to other people's responses. Remarks from others that might be considered merely insensitive by a nontraumatized person can cause sudden and painful secondary wounding to you. Therefore, learn to distance yourself from negative people.

It isn't easy countering the powerful negative messages of secondary wounding, and they will probably always trouble you at times. But as you make progress in finding self-worth and value, you will feel less a victim and more a survivor.

Responses

There are many types of secondary wounding: blaming the survivor, exhibiting ignorance, labeling, and just plain cruelty. Being able to identify the type of remarks made by others will increase your ability to cope in a constructive manner. The pain and humiliation caused by the remark will, of course, still be present, but naming these responses can lessen your secondary wounding.

Here are a few categories of secondary wounding:

- Discounting: Many times people discount the fact that your rape took place, or they minimize it by saying, "It could have been worse. You could have been killed." Remarks like these make the survivor feel guilty, ungrateful, and embarrassed that she even told her story.
- Denial and disbelief: When people say things like, "Oh, come on, that couldn't really have happened," they are not accepting the reality of your trauma.
- Blaming the survivor: Some people talk as though the victim were to blame, at least in part, for what happened. "You probably shouldn't have been there after dark. Maybe it was the dress you were wearing. What about that drink you had?"

- Generalization: One of the social consequences of being traumatized is that the public tends to label you as a victim. People interpret your behavior and emotions in light of that label. For example, "You poor thing."
- Trauma ignorance: Many people have never experienced trauma; therefore, they do not know what to say or do. Some people are fearful when they hear of your rape. It reminds them of their vulnerability to victimization. Some people rattle on, making you feel insignificant and small.
- Cruelty: Secondary wounding almost always feels cruel, even if the other person isn't aware that his or her words are demeaning. Someone hearing of your rape may try to make light of it by telling a rape joke or saying, "Yeah, tell me about it," as if your trauma were a normal occurrence, common to everyone. Our culture has become increasingly emotionally detached, even within the family. Economic and social changes make it difficult for people to empathize with one another.

A further response from both believers and nonbelievers suggests that our faith should protect us from harm. Not so. Walters writes, "Christians are not immune from the misfortunes of life, including sexual violence. Rape, along with life's other tragedies, can happen to anyone. The providence of God does not always spare Christians from life's adversities. Suffering is a universal experience bore by both the godly and the wicked. The Bible doesn't say that nothing bad will ever happen to us. But it does say, in Romans 8:35–39, that nothing that does happen to us can ever separate us from the love of God."[1] You might even remind these people that the apostle Paul, as well as other apostles and disciples, had pretty strong faith but was not immune to harm and, in fact, suffered a great deal of bodily harm.

Recovery

It's important to the healing process to have people come alongside you. Unfortunately, sometimes people do more harm than good. Secondary wounding occurs when people who do not understand your situation are unintentionally cruel.

Family, friends, and professionals are often cruel as well. They can make you feel stupid or ashamed for having been raped. They wonder why you're having such severe reactions to the event and question why you would seek help. People who have never been traumatized have difficulty understanding victims and tend to lack patience with them. Thus the very ones we turn to for emotional support are sometimes the ones who let us down.

Those who do understand and support you, though, are like a lifeline when you're drowning. It's normal for you to grasp at those lifelines in the exhaustion associated with trauma and its aftermath of swirling emotions. Linda Ledray, in her book *Recovering from Rape*, writes,

> We all have only a certain amount of energy available for dealing with stressful events in our lives. Dealing with rape uses up a lot of that energy, so we don't have much left over.
>
> . . . The experience of having your case go to court is another stress for you and for all your friends and family. Years of studies and research in all types of crises, including rape, show that next to your own resilience, the key factor in your recovery is support from family and friends. This is a time of turmoil. You are afraid you'll never recover, but you will.[2]

QUESTIONS TO ANSWER

1. Has someone made hurtful remarks to you? What were they? How did they make you feel?
2. Explain your secondary wounding attitude after your rape

and what that attitude is like now. Has your attitude changed toward society, church, or types/groups of people? Has your attitude changed toward family, friends, or others? Has your attitude affected your ability to participate in clubs, associations, and public activities?

3. How do you plan to overcome secondary wounding?

chapter 18

They Do It Because They Want To

We are the only creatures on the planet that hunt and kill for pleasure and sport.

—Sean Mactire

Rape is a crime of violence. This type of violence is a disease referred to in medical terms as "intentional trauma."[1] It is not a social or a legal problem but a complication of mental illness. Criminals are evil, as we have discovered, who have a constant desire to be childishly self-indulgent. A criminal wishes to do whatever he/she pleases, with nothing but contempt and total disregard for the rights and feelings of others. Like a child, the criminal always wants something for nothing.[2]

Freud once said that a child with power would destroy the world. Simply, a child is totally subjective. A child has no desire to consider, nor accept, the viewpoint of others because a child is incapable of acknowledging anything other than his/her desires or feelings. In his book *Malicious Intent*, Sean Mactire says that the criminal is a ruthless adult who never stops behaving like a child, and who has a chronic obsession with taking shortcuts: "The criminal stagnated in perpetual childhood. This degeneration in behavior is accentuated by three basic traits that signify the criminal personality: (a) weakness, emotional and/or physical, lacking discipline; (b) immaturity, childish egocentrism; (c) self-deception, distorted sense of personal reality, severely narcissistic."[3]

While it's true that everyone is capable of committing a crime, why do some people become diseased with violence and others remain healthy? Mactire says,

> Crime is part of a disease cycle that is infectious; it can be anywhere. With their sheer numbers alone, violent criminals, career criminals, and killers of all types are a society and race unto themselves.
>
> The reality is that all destructive or nonproductive behavior is motivated by power. In a nutshell, crime is about power. In the simplest of terms, criminals are parasites.
>
> Criminals seem to feed on the fear of their victims, feed on the power they derive from their acts, and feed on the pleasure, often sexual, that their acts provide.[4]

America has one of the highest rates of rape in the world.[5] It seems to be the all-American crime. Further, rape is the only crime where the victim is ever regarded as the offender and the only crime for which provocation is often presented as an acceptable defense for the perpetrator. No wonder women are always looking over their shoulders. Going out after dark becomes a serious issue. Running in the park, even with other people, can leave you feeling guarded. Walking up deserted stairs or stepping into an elevator with a solitary man may become a debatable decision.

Liz Kelly, in her book *Surviving Sexual Violence*, says, "Women have to find ways of managing the threat of sexual violence. We choose from a range of coping strategies, each of which involves an assessment of risks and costs. The reality of sexual violence remains such a common experience and while women feel that they can expect little protection from others, be they passersby or the police, a sense of vulnerability is a realistic response. It is one of the many costs of this reality that some women are affected so strongly that they chose to limit their lives in dramatic ways."[6]

Men are not usually threatened with evil by women and children. In daily life they rarely have to look over their shoulders, keeping watch for an unseen enemy. They leave home, have fun, work, and do all the things men like to do without any anxiety. If men could walk in the shoes of women and children for a year, they might have greater understanding about our concerns for safety. A world without rape would be a world where women would be free from the fear of men.

warning signs

Marc MacYoung and Dianna Gordon MacYoung offer a list of behaviors that may identify a potential rapist.[7] If you see the following behaviors in a person, take care. The more of these behaviors you see, the more care should be taken not to be alone with him. Even if he doesn't rape, these behaviors indicate serious character flaws.

- Insensitivity for others/emphasis on self: Does this person put his wants above the needs, feelings, or well-being of others? Such a person has no understanding that he must coexist with others.
- Belittling behavior or attitudes toward others: Does this person habitually make nasty, belittling, or degrading comments about others—especially under the guise of joking? Does this person think he is better than others? A person who feels superior, often assumes the right to "take" what he wants.
- Negating behavior or comments: Comments like "you don't

really mean that" are serious indicators of someone trying to negate you. A person who negates others is trying to take away the other person's thoughts, feelings, and needs and is attempting to project his wants onto that person.

- Hostile and/or threatening language: Choice of words convey subconscious assumptions about a particular topic. Someone who habitually uses violent or threatening language should be carefully watched for possible escalation.
- Bullying: A bully uses the threat of violence more than actual violence. Most often bullies are not willing to risk conflict with someone who can hurt them (an alpha male), and will instead choose to intimidate someone he considers weaker and safer.
- Excessive anger: How easily does this person anger? Does he boil over at the slightest problem? This is an indication of chronic anger. Often people having chronic anger look for targets upon whom to vent their anger.
- Brooding/revenge: Does this person hang onto his anger long after the situation is over? Will he insist on taking revenge for real or imagined slights? A brooder fixates on something and then works himself into a frenzy over it. A person who seeks revenge "has to win" and is willing to take it to extremes. Refusing such a person's sexual advances can turn this tendency toward you.
- Obsession: This is the person who won't leave you alone. He insists on "hitting on you" long after you have told him no. He is always trying to force intimacy. Such obsessions turn into anger when his advances are rejected.
- Extreme mood swings: Beware of someone who can go from wildly happy to deeply wounded at a moment's notice. This sort of personality can feel justified to commit an unlimited amount of violence and damage because you "hurt his feelings."

- Physical tantrums: Beware of a person who regularly physically assaults his environment (e.g., hitting walls, kicking things, etc.). It is only a short step from striking a car to attacking you.
- Jock or gorilla mentality: This mentality is especially common among participants of contact sports. The "jock" receives not only positive reinforcement, but applause for being aggressive and violent. This can easily lead to a failure to differentiate between the playing field and real life.
- A mean drunk: Nearly all rape and abuse cases involve alcohol. Watch what surfaces when someone is intoxicated. It shows what is always lurking underneath. Do not put yourself in a situation where you would deal with such a person while he is intoxicated. Most importantly, don't allow yourself to be diminished by your use of alcohol or drugs in this person's presence.
- Alcohol or drug abuse: Alcohol and drugs are not the cause of bad behavior; they are an excuse! Often an attacker intentionally becomes intoxicated to ignore the social restrictions and inhibitions regarding violence.

Do not ignore or rationalize these behaviors, especially if you see a significant number of them. These danger signals are real. People who rape have long shown a consistent pattern of attitude and behavior. Do not put yourself in a situation where such a person could successfully use violence.

Rapist Profiles

There are six types of rapists: power reassurance, power assertive, anger retaliatory, anger excitation (or the criminal sexual sadist), opportunistic, and gang rapist. Robert Hazelwood, a retired FBI agent, gave the following information on the six types of perpetrators.[8]

Power Reassurance

This is the most common and least violent stranger-to-stranger rapist. He doesn't like what he is doing. His purpose is to reassure himself of his own masculinity. He is highly ritualistic, having no intent to punish or degrade his victim, and is verbally and sexually unselfish. He uses the surprise approach, with a minimal level of force, and preselects victims through window-peeping surveillance. The victim will be in his own age range, and he attacks between midnight and five AM. He attacks victims in their own homes. The victim will remove her own clothing, and the sexual assault will take up a small portion of the time. He will most likely contact his victim again.

He has low self-esteem, is an underachiever, nonathletic, solitary, takes little pride in appearance, collects nonviolent pornography, works in a job with little contact with the public, and is unhappily married or in an unhappy relationship. This type can be treated.

Power Assertive

This is the second most common and third most violent. He is the date rapist. Very impulsive, he asserts his masculinity and feels it is his right to force women to have sex. He is verbally abusive, sexually selfish, manipulative, and exerts a moderate level of force. The victim will be in his own age range.

Assaults will take place away from where he lives or works. He will tear a victim's clothing off, rape the victim more than once, and rely on his fists for weapons. He wants to be viewed as a man's man. He is athletic, exercises regularly, drives a truck, may dress like a cowboy, loves to drink, and hangs out at bars. He takes pride in his personal appearance, is self-centered, and does not like authority figures. He will have a macho job, like construction, and will have multiple marriages. Successful treatment is marginal.

Anger Retaliatory

This is the third most common and second most violent. His purpose is to punish and degrade women, getting even for real or imagined wrongs. He is verbally abusive, sexually selfish, uses the blitz-style approach (sudden and violent), and uses excessive levels of force. The victim will be his age or older (but not the aged). He has no geographic or time pattern. He will rip/tear the victim's clothing off in the areas of assault, and he drinks prior to the assault. He has an explosive temper, abuses alcohol, and has a history of violence against women. He has a dark side, is a lone wolf, and untrusting. He lacks a sense of humor, is a high school dropout, and has multiple marriages. Successful treatment is marginal.

Anger Excitation or the criminal sexual sadist

These men are sexually aroused by the suffering of victims and need to have complete mastery over another person.

They use a con approach, carefully planning their assault and using advanced selection of location for the assault. They intentionally torture their victims, who will be strangers. They approach under a pretext in order to get victims to participate. They beat their victims and keep them captive in sexual bondage. They tell victims to speak in a degrading manner. This perpetrator can be a murderer/serial killer, and he keeps personal items belonging to victims.

He is intelligent, is the most manipulative, the biggest liar, and a boaster. He may be an established solid citizen, unemotional, and unable to feel love. He is a sex dominant. He will become an expert on the subject, inflicting physiological and physical pain. His main preference is anal rape, and he maintains collections of violent themes.

His personality disorders include narcissism. He is grandiose, with a sense of entitlement, and is hypersensitive to criticism. He is antisocial, showing no remorse, no capacity for empathy for others, no conscience, and not able to form lasting relationships. He is paranoid, suspicious, rigid, lacks humor, and puts the blame on others.

This is the least common and most violent, and successful treatment is unlikely.

opportunistic

The opportunistic rapist typically assaults as an afterthought during the commission of another crime. For instance, a burglar who discovers a female alone after he enters a residence, finds her sexually attractive, and impulsively assaults her is an opportunistic rapist. One must not confuse this offender with the burglar who consistently rapes during other crimes. The opportunistic rapist generally uses a minimal level of force and spends a relatively short period of time with the victim, often leaving her bound when he departs. He is sexually and verbally selfish and frequently drinks or consumes drugs prior to the crime.

Gang Rapist

Gang rape involves two or more rapists. Usually there is one leader and possibly one reluctant person involved in a group of three or more persons. This person indicates to the victim he doesn't really want the rape to happen. The assault is completely selfish in nature, but the force level varies from minimal to brutal.

Marital Rape

Marital rape is unwanted intercourse or penetration obtained by force, threat of force, or when the wife is unable to consent. Linda Mintle writes, "Marital rape is a real but controversial subject among many today. . . . There are those who believe that marital rape isn't even possible. These people often view women as property or objects, and feel that married men are entitled to sex no matter what the resistance."[9] Marital rape became a crime in all fifty states on July 5, 1993. Dari Sweeton writes, "It's naïve to assume that marital rape is somehow a less traumatic form of sexual violence than other forms. However, if we take a moment to recognize the extreme betrayal involved when a husband, whose role is to love, cherish, shelter, and provide, violates his wife through sexual violence, we cannot help but be in deep mourning for the devastation to her heart, mind, and soul."[10] Clearly a husband who violates his wife in such a way has problems similar to those of other types of rapists.

*   *   *

Within the profiles of the rapists are the admitters and the deniers. Deniers do not take responsibility for their actions. They sometimes acknowledge their acts, but justify them with excuses: "She was a loose woman." "She enjoyed it." "She was a prostitute." "She was drunk." All refuse accountability and minimize their violence.

The typical rapist is nothing more than an aggressive, hostile person who never grew up and chooses to do violence.

QUESTIONS TO ANSWER

1. What profile best fits your rapist?
2. Did you report your assault?
3. Was your perpetrator convicted of his crime and sentenced to prison?
4. How do you feel about the treatment the rapist received?

where's god?

Be not overcome by evil, but overcome evil with good.
—Romans 12:21 (KJV)

Many Christian women assume they have divine protection from sexual assault. Rape is rarely discussed at their churches, leading these women to believe only unbelievers or backsliders are assaulted. When a Christian woman is raped, she may wonder if God is punishing her. Her friends and family may wonder if her assault is due to past sins. A sexual assault can leave a woman's faith shattered.

When tragedy invades our lives with no apparent or immediate purpose or explanation, we tend to wonder why God allowed it. We sometimes believe God doesn't care about us. But God is a loving, righteous God—kind, perfect, holy, and always does what is good and right. Though we won't always have the answer to *why*, we can be assured of God's compassion. He will lead us out of the darkness of sorrow into the light of acceptance.

The community of Faith

A Christian victim may have to overcome other believers' inappropriate responses to suffering. Many people stifle the efforts of a believer to express negative thoughts or feelings. As Walters writes, "This is particularly damaging to a survivor of rape. Not many understand how she truly feels. They discount the seriousness of her assault. She may be urged to praise God when she feels abandoned by Him. She may be offered Bible verses and platitudes, which sound cruel and superficial to her. She may be pressured to carry on as if everything is normal when, in fact, her world has fallen apart."[1]

Even though some Christians may hurt you unintentionally, it's important to surround yourself with believers who have shown they can minister to you in prayer and comfort.

Larry Crabb says, in his book *Connecting,*

> Ordinary people have the power to change other people's lives. . . . The power is found in connection, that profound meeting when the truest part of one soul meets the emptiest recesses in another and finds something there, when life passes from one to the other. The power to meaningfully change lives depends not on advice . . . but on connecting, on bringing two people into an experience of shared life. . . .
>
> We were designed to connect with others. . . .
>
> Tears without an audience, without someone to hear and care, leave the wounds unhealed. When someone listens to our groanings and stays there, we feel something change inside us. Despair seems less necessary; hope begins to stir where before there was only pain. . . .
>
> Connecting begins when we enter the battle for someone's soul. It continues as we prayerfully envision what Christ would look like in that person's life. It climaxes when the life of Christ within us is released, when something wonderful and alive and good pours out of us to touch the heart of another.[2]

As the writer of Ecclesiastes said, "Two are better than one. . . . If one falls down, his friend can help him up. But pity the man who falls and has no one to help him up!" (4:9–10).

The word of God

Where is God? He comforts you in the words of crisis counselors, in the prayers and nurturing of your brothers and sisters in Christ. He gives you hope and peace in nature—in flowers and birds, in pets and wildlife. He offers advice through those who write books. And He reveals His nature in His Word. Walters writes,

> The Word of God has an amazing transforming capacity to renew and restore. Following the desolation of a sexual attack, your substance and stability can hinge on reading, meditating on, and memorizing meaningful Bible verses.
>
> If you have difficulty reading the Bible because you are still too angry or confused, Christian music, tapes, or literature can revive your spirit. However, some victims will need more time than others before they are open to any kind of spiritual nourishment.[3]

It's tempting to make your sexual assault a permanent disability. But surely you don't want to disable yourself that way. Only God knows what good things you have yet to offer to others. Yes . . . you have faced suffering in this life—we all do—but God can bring hope and restoration into the worst circumstances. He is able to turn evil into good (Gen. 50:20), and we can eventually find meaning in our pain. Though our sorrow is heavy to bear, the strength we gain from carrying it will not be wasted. As humans, we find it easy to see nothing redemptive in our trauma, but God can use our afflictions to draw us close to Him and through us to reveal His awesomeness to an unbelieving world.

QUESTION TO ANSWER

If God wrote a letter to you, what do you think He would say to console you? Listen for that still, small voice whispering to your spirit. Write such a letter to yourself from God or copy the following letter and frame it for a constant reminder of God's love. Here is what one woman wrote:

My child,

I have waited for you. You have no idea how precious you are to Me. I've been with you all along, hurting when you hurt, wanting to offer comfort, and rejoicing when you have rejoiced, even if for wrong reasons.

You are one whom I have created, and I've been wanting to raise you up in all the glories I have for you. I know it is difficult to understand, but try to participate in this truth. I love you so much that I will not violate your essence by taking away your will or forcing My ways on you. I have respected the choices of man, releasing him to his choices for a set season. All offenses will one day be set right.

I do not wish for any of My children to hurt. Yet I am Justice and I am Mercy. I am big enough to allow time for repentance for the offender, as well as to heal and comfort the offended. I have not left either without what they need.

All you will ever need is here if you will just believe I have it for you and ask. I will not force anything upon you, as man forces his will on you. I love you.

I am pleased with My creation and I will move heaven and earth to reestablish you to health, wholeness, peace, joy, and serenity. Look to Me; let Me show you the master copy of your existence. You will see the beauty I see. Let Me love you and heal your wounds. I love you, My child—I do . . . God

—Ann[4]

chapter 20

Relationship Effects

A sorrow that is shared is cut in half; a joy that is shared is doubled.

—St. Aelred of Rievaulx

Divorce: A Side Effect of Rape

"Eighty percent of marriages don't survive a rape," a counselor told Patricia Weaver Francisco, author of *Telling: A Memoir of Rape and Recovery*.[1] It is common for couples to divorce after the rape of a spouse. Rape pulls hard on the links that hold a marriage together. A myriad of adverse circumstances that are just a part of the aftermath of rape can weaken the links, making divorce inevitable. Divorce, however, is often no relief. It is often a long, painful process that never seems to end. Pursued by memory and attachment (children), along with unrelenting guilt, the rape survivor still feels wounds that continue to fester.

It needs to be understood that husbands, too, suffer the consequences of rape. The initial response by a husband in the first three months after his wife has been raped is crucial. Does he see her as a victim who has been hurt, or does he associate the rape with character flaws in her? Does he see the rape as an act of sex or an act of violence?

Some husbands resort to "if I" language: "If I had only [fill in the blank], maybe it wouldn't have happened." They also cope with their anger by aiming it at the perpetrator: "I'll kill him if I get a hold of him!" These feelings of "if only" and "I'll kill him" are all part of the psychological impact of rape on a husband. His wife's rape is something a husband is never prepared for. Still, he must find ways to cope with stressful situations. His wife will likely have new phobias. Conversations about the rape, which many couples avoid, will no doubt be strained and awkward. Going to court with his wife and facing the rapist will arouse passions so intense they may take the husband by surprise. Resuming sexual relations could be a struggle; the wife is now extremely phobic over sex, and the husband has a hard time thinking about sex with his wife after her rape.

Because America is such a transient country, friends and family who would normally provide emotional support can be scattered, thus the burden is often left to the husband and wife alone. Many times the husband's reactions leave him incapable of supporting her.

In my self-absorption following my rape, I didn't consider my former husband's struggle to understand what was happening to us. Prior to our divorce, the layers of damage from my rape were never repaired. I became a different person as the aftermath was too much for me. I couldn't think, I couldn't cope, I needed time. Like two shipwrecks at sea, we kept colliding, and then we silently drifted away from each other. Following the divorce, memories and attachment, along with unrelenting guilt, continued to fester in me.

other men

After my rape, I became suspicious of every man I met. My thoughts were extremely unkind. *He probably rapes his wife every night. He's probably a registered sex offender. He probably molests his children.* Every man became a suspect. Man was the hunter, and like an endangered species, I was the game.

I also became suspicious of men wanting to befriend my children. "I'll drop the girls off for you." *Over my dead body!* I didn't overprotect my children, but I didn't let them run, willy-nilly, with just any man.

Everyday occurrences became possible dangers: *Is it safe for the girls to walk to the mailbox out of sight six blocks away, with no neighbors in sight? Is it safe for the girls to wait for the bus in the same location by themselves? Is it safe for them to stay overnight with a friend? What if the father molests them?* Terror seemed to lurk everywhere.

In time . . . a lot of time . . . years and years of time . . . I became less fearful, but remained cautious. I'm still suspicious of some men, but I trust God to give me discernment so I no longer act like a half-crazed woman.

Friends

After a rape, it's very possible that your friendships will be affected. Part of that is because some friends don't know what to say or how to act around someone who's been raped. And part of it is because the survivor is a changed person who thinks differently than she used to.

For many women, the thought of telling others about their rape seals their lips. Some don't even tell their husbands, even if the assault happened while they were married. I was reluctant to tell friends. Was I afraid of embarrassing them? Was I afraid of being questioned? Was I ashamed of what I didn't have any control over? Perhaps they'd feel sorry for me, and I didn't want pity.

After I told one woman about my rape, she said, "I'm so sorry that happened to you." I'm sure she really meant it. Then she added, "Why don't you take a cruise? It will make you feel better," as if getting over rape is the same as getting over the flu.

I told a few close girlfriends who lived out-of-town. I told no one at church. Friends and family were so scattered that it was impossible to stay connected to one support person. There were no rape crisis centers, no rape hotlines, virtually no books on rape recovery, and no Christian counseling centers anywhere close to me.

I felt sealed in silence.

Everyone is unique, however, and every raped woman reacts differently about sharing her devastating news. But you need to tell someone. Without emotional support, hope is lost. When hope is lost, the reason to live dies.

After my rape, I wasn't who I was. I became a different person. I wasn't broken . . . I was shattered. I needed a friend to help me put the pieces back together, and that didn't happen.

So it was just me and God. I felt the Holy Spirit whisper, "He heals the brokenhearted and binds up their wounds" (Ps. 147:3). And He has.

Yes, with God, you can recover from rape even without the help of others. It just takes longer.

QUESTIONS TO ANSWER

1. Were you aware of your husband's struggles prior to your divorce (if you're divorced)?
2. Did your husband see your rape as an act of sex or as an act of violence?
3. Do you find yourself overly suspicious of men?
4. Did you share your rape experience with friends? If not, why not?
5. Do you have at least one person with whom you can share in confidence?

chapter 21

Marital Intimacy After Rape

Who is this coming up from the desert leaning on her lover?
—Song of Songs 8:5

"Can I experience marital intimacy after rape?" you ask. You can if you and your husband are willing to be patient and to communicate. Remember, though, that intimacy is more than sex. Intimacy is sharing on a deeply personal level with your spouse and is like two people singing in harmony, each understanding the words and the tune in the same way. Couples can experience intimacy preparing a meal together, painting a room together, or laughing together at a favorite video.

Regaining sexual intimacy in marriage after a rape, though, requires a few things. First you must trust God. He was there when you were assaulted, and He grieved for you. Though it was not His will, He desires to make something beautiful of it. In time, He will show you how your rape experience can help others. This may not sound comforting to you right now, but hang in there. Your sorrow will not be wasted.

Next, you'll have to be open and honest with your husband. When you talk and share openly with him, you're inviting him into your life, seeking comfort from him. After all, he's going through this recovery mess, too. Most husbands want to help; they just don't know how.

Regaining sexual intimacy depends, too, on the state of your marriage before your rape. Was your marriage strong? Was your marriage on the rocks? If it was rocky, did you and your husband seek marital counseling? If so, was your relationship improving? If not, your rape experience can shatter your marriage.

Were you a victim of incest, molestation, or other sexual assaults in the past? If so, did you receive therapy at that time to overcome the negative effects? If not, your rape experience may impede your recovery as well as the recovery of your marriage.

If you can't discuss your rape with your husband, sexual activities should be postponed temporarily. If you do resume sexual intimacy, stop if you're fearful, nauseated, crying, dissociating, feeling trapped, ashamed, having flashbacks, or unable to take joy in the experience. Don't grin and bear it. Before you were raped, you may sometimes have had sex with your husband, without being totally engaged, simply because you wanted to please him. There's nothing wrong with that, and it is, in fact, a giving and loving thing to do. But after a rape, your body remembers the attack, causing you to react negatively. Unengaged sex now feels totally different, and rather than your feeling giving, you may feel used.

Because healing is an ongoing process, one day you may feel affectionate and the next recoil at a gentle hug. Let your husband know how you're feeling. It's all right to request that your husband ask you first before touching you intimately. Make sure he understands that you're not rejecting *him*, but that his patience, understanding, and willingness to stop will help you recover faster and fuller. When you're ready to make love again, tell him or show him.

Your need to be in control is natural at this stage of recovery. While you may not be ready for sexual activity, you may want other forms of physical contact such as hand holding, kisses, hugs, and snuggling on the sofa. Other ways your husband can show care for you are by walking together on the beach or anywhere, taking in a movie, surprising you with a picnic, or cooking your favorite meal. A weekend away together can create a serene opportunity for intimacy.

If you're still having problems with sexual intimacy, perhaps you *and* your husband should seek professional counseling, preferably with someone specializing in rape recovery and sex therapy. The more your husband knows what to expect and how to handle the aftermath of spousal rape, the quicker recovery will be for both of you.

Regaining sexual intimacy in your marriage can be a lifelong roller-coaster ride, but if your expecting ups and downs, discouragement won't overcome you. Trust God. He's on that ride with you. He's faithful, true, and just. He's the Deliverer.

If you're sincere in your desire to resume sexual activity with your husband, purchase a card and enclose the following message with a personal note:

- Honor me. That means to be respectful of my wishes, and I will want to be intimate with you.
- Forgive me when I refuse your sexual advances. I'm still processing my thoughts and feelings.
- Love me in spite of my resistance: "Husbands, love your wives and do not be embittered against them" (Col. 3:19 NASB).

Lay the card on top of a box of his favorite candy.

QUESTIONS TO ANSWER

1. How can your husband show you comfort?
2. Are you ready for sexual intimacy? If not, what is your plan to help you move in this direction?

chapter 22

Mother Eve

*I will bring health and healing to [her]; I will heal [her] and will
let [her] enjoy abundant peace and security.*

—Jeremiah 33:6

Genesis gives a majestic account of all that the Creator brought
into being. Genesis takes the reader back to the all-important moment of creation when the omnipotent Creator spoke into existence the matchless wonders of sun, moon, stars, planets, galax-
ies, plants, moving creatures, and man—the one whom He made
in His image.[1]

Man's body was fashioned by the Lord God from the dust of the
ground, while his spirit came from the very "breath" of God. Yet
Moses, the inspired author of Genesis, alluded to man's loneliness
and lack of full satisfaction. But the Creator had not finished. He
had plans for providing a companion who would satisfy the unfulfilled yearning of man's heart, a companion created for fellowship
and companionship.

Jehovah made it possible for man to have a helpmate. She was
to be one who could share man's responsibilities, respond to his
nature with understanding and love, and wholeheartedly cooper-
ate with him in working out the plan of God.[2] Eve was a precious

daughter of God, created in His image, presented to man to be loved, honored, and cherished.

The *Zondervan NIV Matthew Henry Commentary* says, "Woman was taken not from man's head to rule over him, nor from his feet to be trampled on by him, but out of his side to be equal with him, under his arm to be protected, and close to his heart to be beloved."[3] She is also represented in the story of creation as wholly dependent upon her husband, and as man is never fully complete without the woman, she is not complete without him.

The loving heart of God doubtless rejoiced in the institution of a relationship that was to be clean, holy, and pleasant for humankind.[4] And man and woman were intended by God to have intimacy with Him. In the garden of Eden, a quiet place of indescribable beauty, humankind was to enjoy fellowship and companionship with the Creator.[5]

In the middle of the garden was the Tree of Life. Of this tree Adam and Eve might eat and live forever in happiness—even to immortality and everlasting bliss—through the grace and favor of their Maker. God imposed one condition, however—that Adam and Eve persevere in their state of innocence and obedience.

In the garden was also the Tree of Knowledge of Good and Evil, and from that Adam and Eve were not to eat or they would die. That tree, in itself, though, had no virtue to beget or increase useful knowledge. So why did God put that tree in the garden in the first place? The answer is simple: God doesn't want robots for companionship. He gave us free will so that we might choose to love Him. The covenant of innocence had in it not only a positive command, "do this and live," which was sealed and confirmed by the Tree of Life. The covenant also contained a negative command, the consequence of rebelling: "fail this and die," that is, "be separated from God," which was the consequence of eating from the Tree of Knowledge of Good and Evil.

Ellen G. White writes, "God does not force the will or judgment of any. He takes no pleasure in a slavish obedience. He desires that the creatures of His hands shall love Him because He is worthy of love. He would have them obey Him because they have an intelligent appreciation of His wisdom, justice, and benevolence."[6]

Adam and Eve were allowed to choose. Genesis 3:1–5 says,

> Now the serpent was more crafty than any of the wild animals the LORD God had made. He said to the woman, "Did God really say, 'You must not eat from any tree in the garden'?"
>
> The woman said to the serpent, "We may eat fruit from the trees in the garden, but God did say, 'You must not eat fruit from the tree that is in the middle of the garden, and you must not touch it, or you will die.'"
>
> "You will not surely die," the serpent said to the woman. "For God knows that when you eat of it your eyes will be opened, and you will be like God, knowing good and evil."

Eve believed the Serpent, or wanted to believe him, took the fruit, and gave some to her husband, Adam, who was with her. Then their eyes were opened and they realized they were naked. They made inadequate coverings for themselves and hid from God, for they were ashamed.

Humans are now aware of the existence of good and evil. Good is obedience; evil is rebellion. No one *told* Adam and Eve what good and evil are, but once they had rebelled by disobeying, they knew. By the loss of good, we have experiential knowledge of what good is, and by our own sense of moral conscience, we know what evil is.

When confronted by God for their sin, though, neither Adam nor Eve accepted any blame. Instead it was a classic case of "he said, she said." Eve said, "The serpent deceived me, and I ate" (Gen. 3:13). Adam said, "The woman you put here with me—she gave me some fruit from the tree, and I ate it" (Gen. 3:12).

In the end, all of them—the serpent, the man, and the woman—had to suffer the consequences of their own transgressions.

The Lord God said to the serpent, "Because you have done this, cursed are you above all the livestock and all the wild animals! You will crawl on your belly and you will eat dust all the days of your life. And I will put enmity between you and the woman, and between your offspring and hers; he will crush your head, and you will strike his heel" (Gen. 3:14–15).

To the woman He said, "I will greatly increase your pains in childbearing; with pain you will give birth to children. Your desire will be for your husband, and he will rule over you" (Gen. 3:16).

To Adam He said, "Because you listened to your wife and ate from the tree about which I commanded you, 'You must not eat of it,' cursed is the ground because of you; through painful toil you will eat of it all the days of your life. It will produce thorns and thistles for you, and you will eat the plants of the field. By the sweat of your brow you will eat your food until you return to the ground, since from it you were taken; for dust you are and to dust you will return" (Gen. 3:17–19).

Adam and Eve then realized that their intimate connection with God was broken, and a terrible loneliness overwhelmed them. Remorse and its inevitable miseries followed. All humanity henceforth would be doomed to struggle with sin.

Many people believe this story is a myth, made up by certain tribes in early biblical times so they could control women. I believe the Bible is God's truth. Whether you're a believer or a nonbeliever, it's easy to imagine the fights that might have taken place after Adam and Eve were banished from Paradise. He'd blame her for eating the fruit; she'd blame him because he didn't protect her from Satan's temptation.

It's takes no imagination, though, to figure out that some time in the very distant past, men feared the power of women. And woman's power is derived through sex. To control women is to control their power. The experience of Adam and Eve prompted men to "tighten the reins" on women, ensuring that they never again could entice men into a fatal error. Perhaps men believed they could prevent women themselves from stumbling into evil. Regardless, in rebellion and the desire for power, we find the beginning of chauvinistic beliefs and the suppression of women.

Because of sin, God judged not only woman, He pronounced judgment on all creation. Because we know that God is good and just, we must accept God's judgment as right. Not to do so is rebellion toward God. While we cannot fully comprehend the nature of God's judgment, we can understand that rebellion leads to grief and sorrow.

Accepting our divine judgment does not mean women are to be treated violently, verbally abused, raped, cheated on, dishonored, or disrespected. Woman's judgment was not intended to bring her to ruin, but to repentance. The entrance of sin made the world the way it is now, and it's a world in which everyone suffers, a world which otherwise *would not have been*. Rebelling against God's judgment, though, violates and thwarts a divine law and sentence. Considering our crime against God's protective instructions for humanity, the judgment is fair.

Adam and Eve had to suffer the consequences for their disobedience, and so do all men and women. How else will we learn right from wrong and have a desire to do what is good and right? Woman's consequence is subjection to her husband. The subjection, however, was never intended to be misused. Rather it was a reminder to never forget our disobedience.

God's judgment on women does not mean that a woman cannot be a whole, fulfilled person. It means each woman is protected by God and can live unhindered by guilt. Women can aspire to the same things as men—dreams, careers, hobbies, education, owning property and businesses, flying to the moon. Every woman should seek the desires of her heart.

I confess, there was a time when I could not have agreed with this chapter, much less written it. I'd go out of the way to demean men, and in general considered them untrustworthy. A lifetime of harboring a rebellious attitude toward men can be difficult to change. Sometimes my old attitude tries to take over my thoughts, and I have to bite my tongue so I won't say something I'll regret. As I am reminded of God's love, calm and peace fill my heart, making it easier to control my emotions.

QUESTIONS TO ANSWER

1. Do you blame others for your misfortune?
2. Do you harbor rebellious thoughts toward men and those who have hurt you?

chapter 23

A social and cultural crisis

The night is far spent, the day is at hand: let us therefore cast off the works of darkness, and let us put on the armor of light.
—Romans 13:12 (KJV)

In the previous chapter, we talked about God's judgment on Eve in the garden of Eden. She would realize womanly longings and desires, but would be in subjection to the man. Through the ages men have abused this Scripture, twisting it in the name of God's holy Word to subordinate and control women.

It seems that men have been particularly interested in controlling women's sexuality. Long ago, Jewish tradition stated that a woman could not read before men because a woman's voice is a sexual provocation.[1] In centuries past, foot binding was a Chinese ritual, which enforced the chastity of women, since women with bound feet were physically incapable of venturing far from home.[2] In Saudi Arabia, a woman must remain veiled in public. The dress code is designed so that a woman cannot sexually arouse a man she casually passes in the street. Women wear long petticoats over floor-length dresses with long sleeves and high necks. Then they are cloaked in the *abbaaya*, a long, black cloak that extends from head to toe.[3]

You'll notice that all these restrictions have more to do with the insecurities and fears of men rather than with any actual inherent tendency for wrongdoing in women. Throughout history, young males have been presented with the message that real men dominate women. While the vast majority of men have for the most part outgrown these fears and insecurities, a minority of men have a sick need to exert control over women through the crime of rape.

Today, every two minutes, one woman is raped somewhere in the United States. In 2006, 272,350 victims reported sexual assault— and it's estimated that 60 percent of sexual assault cases are not reported to the police. One in six women will be raped at some time during their lives.[4]

This climate of violence leaves women afraid. They fear predators who may be walking the streets, looking very average, like your favorite uncle, your mailman, a teacher or preacher. Women who are educated from infancy to believe that all men are caring and will protect them are in for a rude awakening when they learn that the men they trust can violate them.

Rape, though, is not just a problem for women. It is both a social and a cultural crisis. In the United States, rape is more related to societal ills than it is to culture, yet worldwide, women make up the highest number among the casualties in the war of rape. Under the international rules of war, rape is considered a criminal act and is punishable by death or imprisonment.[5] Yet, as widely reported in the media, during ethnic cleansings thousands of women and young girls are being raped in the name of war. In the name of victory and power, it seems that men feel they are given a license to rape.

Myths and Facts About Rape

Considering the international prohibitions and penalties related to rape, society regardless holds confused attitudes about it. The crime of rape is somewhat unique because it involves the sex act yet in reality has nothing to do with sexual desire. Therefore, many people have a hard time separating the facts about rape from the myths. Many institutions and individuals tend to misplace blame for rape, applying at least part of it to the victim. As a rape survivor, you need to examine the extent to which you yourself have accepted the attitudes of society that blame the victim.

Those attitudes are partly shaped by the myths surrounding rape. Here are a few of them:

- Men rape for sexual release.
- Women enjoy or need a little rape.
- Only young, attractive women get raped.
- You didn't resist, so you must have wanted it.
- Date rape really isn't rape.
- Men don't get raped.

Let's examine these myths one by one. First, rape is not simply sexually motivated. It is not a crime of passion but a crime of violence and aggression, used as a weapon to intimidate, terrorize, control, and humiliate the rape victim and make her fear for her life. Las Vegas, a city surrounded by legalized prostitution, has 1.18 times more rapes per capita than the national average.[6] If a man needed merely sexual release, it is available to him without the use of violence.

Second, no mentally healthy woman wants to be raped. As a woman, you know that you are all about relationship and communication. During rape, a woman's body is merely used for a perpetrator's own reasons. Her very physical and psychological selves are violated in the most personal way possible, without the least bit of thought about her as a person. No woman wants or needs to be violated in that way.

Third, all kinds of women are raped. Old women, women of all sizes, shapes, and degrees of attractiveness are raped. Babies and young children are raped. Rape is most often a crime of opportunity. If a rapist perceives an opportunity to rape, it makes no difference to him what a woman looks like or how old she is. He doesn't care what religion she is, either, or where she's from; Christians and women of all faiths and ethnicities are raped. Nice girls get raped.

Fourth, there are several reasons why some women do not resist rape. Some are afraid that if they resist, they may be murdered. The perpetrator may have threatened to kill the victim, her family, or a beloved pet if she resisted. Others are concerned for their children. The mother fears for their lives, as well as wanting to prevent damaging memories of such horrible assault (such was the case with my rape). Assuredly each victim who did not resist had a good reason for doing so. No woman wants to be raped.

Fifth, men do force sex on their dates. Forced sex is rape. Just because a woman agrees to go on a date with a man does not make it okay for him to rape her.

And yes, men do get raped. The National Center for Victims of Crime report that 3 percent of American men—a total of 2.78 million—have experienced rape.[7] The majority of male victims, 71 percent, were raped before the age of eighteen.[8]

Some of the above myths about rape enable us to believe we live in a just world, and that some rapes are really justified. Other myths allow us to believe we can prevent rapes. We want to believe that a woman won't get raped if she dresses modestly, goes to church every Sunday, minds her own business, and stays away from unsavory places. The fact is more women are raped in their homes than any other place.[9] All these myths are pure fiction and give us a false sense of security.

Women can't be sure, either, they'll be safe with men who don't look like rapists. Rapists may be typical in appearance, looking like any average person. They don't seem to be mentally ill or deranged, and they often know or recognize their victims.[10]

societal views of the victim

"Violence against women is not confined to any particular political or economic system, but is prevalent in every society in the world. It cuts across boundaries of wealth, race, and culture. The power structures within society which perpetuate violence against women are deep-rooted and intransigent. The experience or threat of violence inhibits women everywhere from fully exercising and enjoying their human rights."[11]

As a society we cannot tolerate treating rape and the degradation of women as less than the crime it is. Despite widespread media attention, reformed laws, and increased education and sensitivity, many people don't quite know what to think about sexual assault. Some women are not certain that forced sex is a crime, and for those who do recognize it, many social barriers prevent them from reporting it. The unsympathetic see the rape victim as promiscuous or contaminated, and she is sometimes seen as less than human. Even in our day and age, a stigma of shame is attached to the victim. Unlike any other victim of a violent crime, a rape victim is often categorized as a failure for having been raped. People seem to forget that rape is caused by the rapist, not the victim.[12]

People who view rape as sexual activity rather than violence believe that the rapist is motivated by uncontrollable desire, that the woman is somehow responsible for the attack, and that rape does not hurt the victim any more than sex does. They reason that it isn't a cause for concern, but a subject to shun or to snicker about.[13]

In some African cultures rape is considered a ritual.[14] Rape, however, is not a normal way of relating, regardless of culture or society. "Rape is not a natural act for men. A study by anthropologist Peggy Reeves Sanday found that in cultures with a high incidence of rapes, the economic, religious, and political structures are controlled by men. In Sanday's study of forty-four societies that were not patriarchal, there was virtually no rape."[15]

In the war of rape, though, women are fighting back:

Women throughout the world have organized to expose and counter violence against women. They have achieved dramatic changes in laws, policies, and practices. They have brought the violations out of the shadows and into the spotlight. They have established that violence against women demands a response from governments, communities, and individuals. Above all, they have challenged the view of women as passive victims of violence. Despite the obstacles they face in many countries, women are leading the struggle to prevent violence against women. However, in many countries women's rights activists have been confronted by a "backlash" from forces that see gender equality as a threat to social stability and entrenched economic interests. In parts of the world, gains by women are being reversed or ignored.[16]

The war, then, is not over. There are still battles to fight. As a society, we must be made aware of what rape is and aware of the aftermath suffered by the survivor. Rapists must know that they will without question suffer consequences for their acts.

QUESTIONS TO ANSWER

1. What is your opinion of some of the views held about rape by portions of society? Write down your thoughts.
2. Can you read about wounded women without hardening your heart? If not, what steps can you take to free yourself of this feeling?

chapter 24

victim Thinking

The longer we dwell on our misfortunes, the greater is their power to harm us.

—Voltaire

Victim thinking is acting as though the assault is still happening. Your rape may be over, but it is still the dominant event in your life. This kind of victim mentality can lead to a *martyr complex*, which is constantly living with a feeling of great suffering. Continually focusing on your pain can lead to criticizing yourself and others.

But you need not spend the rest of your life thinking like a victim. Fear, anger, and grief need not have a stronghold on your life. You can take back control over your thoughts. Emotional healing comes by speaking positive and encouraging words to yourself and others.

Here are a few victim thoughts:

- Nobody will want me. I'm tarnished.
- I can't trust anyone anymore.
- I feel people are always looking at me, like "raped" is written on my forehead.
- The future scares me.

- I feel guilty.
- I will never get over this.

We need to fight aggressively against victim thinking. You have the opportunity to make for yourself a productive, positive future. God has given you a chance to start over, to find a new identity, to view your world in a beautiful, unexpected way.

Restructuring Your Life

Rape changes your perception of life. What once seemed important may hold little value now. When something as traumatic as rape occurs, survivors are given the opportunity to make positive changes in their lives. While this can be challenging, it is possible. With good counseling, friends, support groups, and sound coping strategies, you can begin the process of restructuring your life.

Having a positive view of yourself is helpful in the restructuring process. Your willingness to heal is apparent by the fact that you're reading this book, and as you move through the process of healing, you forge a new self. Here's a metaphor that works for me: A crystal glass is shattered and then painstakingly put back together, piece by piece, with lead cames holding the fragments.[1] The original material is thus molded into a goblet of a much different design, strength, and beauty.[2]

Many women think they will never recover from rape. While it's natural for a victim to feel that way at first, if she maintains that thinking for too long, it becomes another means Satan uses to further destroy her life. Candace Walters writes,

> Remember that you are wounded, not dead. And for every wound there is a healing process. . . . There is the tendency to think that rape is the one insurmountable problem outside of God's intervention. While rape is probably man's foulest outrage against a fellow human being, there is no

situation where God is not involved and concerned. God hates all evil, especially rape. When His children suffer, He also suffers. However disgusting or shattering your circumstance, God has the power to repair and restore.[3]

Thinking Positively

What is the positive side to your rape?

You're probably stunned by such a question, but out of every trial comes enrichment. We need to reclaim some of what was lost by discovering what we have gained, thereby transforming the negative into something positive. For example, you may learn compassion for others, be able to reevaluate your goals and values, or discover strength you didn't know you had.

List some new and positive discoveries you've made about yourself since your rape. Describe what you've gained in place of your loss. Here are some positive things that I've gained since I was raped:

- I have a closer relationship with God.
- I've developed compassion for others.
- I value some things in my life less, like possessions and reading magazines, and value other things more. Family, friends, and the Word of God now occupy my time.
- I cherish life more abundantly.
- I have a greater appreciation for God's beautiful world.
- My writing has gained strength.
- I have a new appreciation for men. (Yes, I know that sounds strange!)
- I've gotten rid of a lot of my old bad attitudes.

Learn to take control of runaway thoughts that dominate your mind. When intrusive thoughts of your rape flood your mind, stop and say, "It's all over. I'm safe now. He's nowhere near." As you restructure your life, fear, anger, self-blame, and your blaming of others will have less control over you.

Now, say this out loud: "This is the last time I will ever think negative thoughts about myself. I choose to fight against victim thinking."

QUESTIONS TO ANSWER

1. Who were you before the rape? A little girl, a mother, home-maker, career woman? What did your days hold? Did you play, garden, have hobbies, pursue outside interests, volunteer, or serve in the church or community?

2. What changed after your sexual assault? Did you withdraw, quit your job or volunteering, lose interest in hobbies, or isolate yourself?

3. Can you name anything positive you have gained as a result of your rape?

4. What victim thoughts, if any, do you still harbor?

chapter 25

Releasing Your Anger

In your anger do not sin.

—Ephesians 4:26

Ephesians 4:26 says that emotional anger is not wrong. It's what we do with the anger that determines whether it is good or bad. After a rape, it's normal at first to feel rage, hate, and bitterness toward the rapist. If these feelings persist, however, it will hinder your recovery. Instead of letting yourself get to the stage of exploding, share your feelings with an uninvolved party and with God.

One way of releasing pent-up anger is to "speak" to the rapist. Buried feelings surface when you can write in vivid detail about your sexual assault. Letter writing is a safe way of releasing bottled-up emotions of anger, bitterness, sadness, hate, unforgiveness, and fear.

Write a letter to your rapist. Tell him who you were before the rape, and how your life changed after the rape. Express the intensity of the emotions he left you with. Naming these emotions will help lead you to healing and resolution. Take as much time as you need, in one sitting or over a period of time. Say the following prayer before you write:

Heavenly Father God,
I come before You once again with shaky feelings of fear, sadness, and anger. Guide my hands as I write to the evil one who shattered my life. Banish the shadows of hate. Clothe me with forgiveness. Help me to see the perpetrator through the eyes of Jesus that I might stand before You someday, grateful for learning Your ways. In Jesus' name, amen.

When you have finished your letter, you may mail it to the rapist (yes, even if it was your father), throw it away, or tuck in a drawer. I suggest you keep a copy to read in the future. You'll be surprised at how much you've healed since the day you wrote it. There will come a time when you'll read the letter and not feel any of the bitter emotions you once felt. You may want to bury or burn the original copy later as a final act of grieving. Then write a letter or poem of gratitude to God—for creating you, for the special people in your life, for being alive, for His presence, for whatever else that is important to you.

The following letter is a good example of a letter from a survivor.[1] Charlotte's bad feelings about her abuser is evident, but with time she may come to forgive him.

Homer:
You are one of the most vile creatures I have ever encountered. Why did you violate the role of being a stepfather? You were emotionally, physically, and sexually abusive to everyone in the home. You schemed and groomed us with sexual pornography and other sick literature.

Your face, your touches, your words have haunted me over the years. My emotional pain, the deep betrayal, the disgust that I carried should have killed me. But what they did was push me into the safety of God's arms. Oh, the joy of knowing and loving Him.

You had only a season of my life, implanting destruction.
In His hands, betrayal becomes construction . . . building
wondrous things in me. The power you had over me is broken because of Jesus. I now have a life that lasts past time,
knowing restoration, salvation, healing, and true abiding
love. In His hands, perversion dies and truth prevails. In
His hands, pain becomes praise. Death within me is now
abundant life!

Glory to God forever!

Charlotte

We cannot hang on to the past as an excuse for justifying our
present anger. How does holding on to the past serve any positive
purpose?

Confess your anger to God and ask Him to help you resolve it.
You may have repressed anger or bitter feelings toward Him. You
reason that if He is really God and truly benevolent, He wouldn't
have allowed this to happen to one of His children. You may feel
that God has abandoned you. In addition, you may think that a
God who is most often characterized as male cannot understand
a woman's victimization. You might believe his "maleness" makes
Him an accomplice to the crime.[2]

You don't have to be afraid God will punish you if you've been
angry at Him. He is a Father, after all, and He understands that
His children sometimes vent their anger. While anger toward God
is sometimes a normal reaction, it's always undeserving, since He
claims in Psalm 103 to be perfectly fair, righteous, and loving in all
that He does. He is never withdrawn or indifferent. In Isaiah 43:2
God promises to be with us in our suffering.

Confess your anger toward God—and others—and ask His help
to resolve it—not for His sake, but for yours.[3]

QUESTIONS TO ANSWER

1. Are you still angry at your rapist?
2. What do you do with your anger?
3. Have you written a letter to your rapist or to those who have hurt you?

chapter 26

DO WE EVEr rECOVEr?

You will go out in joy and be led forth in peace. . . . Instead of the thornbush will grow the pine tree, and instead of briers the myrtle will grow.

—Isaiah 55:12–13

Courtenay Harding of Boston University asked a number of re-covered schizophrenics, "What really made the difference in your recovery?" Most said something about a person who told them that they have a chance to get better. "Having someone believe in them translated into hope. Without hope, death can establish a foothold. Hope fights fear and nurtures courage. It inspires vi-sion."[1] Hope is essential to beginning the work required to realize what seems unattainable.

You may ask, "Will I ever recover?" The answer is yes, but it's wishful thinking to set a timeline on your recovery. Recovery comes gradually, a little like a physical wound that heals. You don't actually feel a cut healing, but one day you notice that the wound looks a lot better, and you think, *Huh. When did that happen?*

Everyone recovers differently, though, and at a different rate. Full recovery may even be a lifetime process. Just when we think we've left the negative emotions behind, something happens and those feelings overtake us again. But we can get a second wind by remembering how far we've come.

Progress in healing comes from maturing in our thinking and a turnaround in our perception. Perception is, in fact, a key in recovery. I mentioned in a previous chapter that our attitudes are the way we perceive reality. When our perceptions are negative, our attitudes are all negative. That's why it isn't the trauma itself that sends us into a spin, but rather our perception of it.

By allowing God to change your perception, you can learn to deal with intrusive negative thoughts of the past by replacing them with positive ones. This is where positive self-talk comes into play. Self-talk includes making a positive *choice* to heal. Here's a sequence of actions you can accomplish by positive self-talk:

ACCEPT. I choose to accept the fact that I cannot undo the reality of what has taken place in my life, but with God's help, I can change the *effect* it has on me.

AGREE. I choose to agree to live with the consequences of someone else's sin.

BELIEVE. I choose to believe that God's unfailing love for me can deliver me from all my wounds and the strongholds of pain.

CHANGE. Negative thinking leads to wrong behavior, producing rebellious actions. I can change my behavior by allowing God to address my bad attitude.

DEAL. I choose to deal with strongholds of the past by letting go of anger, bitterness, contempt, and unforgiveness.

LISTEN. I choose to accept the past with an open heart by listening to God. Listening is being obedient.

FEAR NOT. I cannot eliminate the cause of fear, but I don't have to let it control me.

FORGIVE. I choose to relent to a teachable spirit and forgiving heart. Forgiveness is done not for God but for me.

It begins with a decision, a choice. The feeling that I *have* forgiven will follow, sooner or later.

TELL. I will tell my story, bringing hope and healing to others as well as myself.

You might say, "I've gone through recovery programs. Why don't I feel healed? I expected big changes to take place." Don't despair. You'll recover from your sexual assault. Understanding your biochemistry (pp. 101–2) and what you have learned in this book will form the basis for continued healing in the months ahead. The process of your healing will come gradually as you are able to change and adapt to a different you.

Recovery comes by learning how to forgive, by understanding evil, and by the willingness to trust God for your recovery. The same maturing, understanding, and trusting that brought us this far will take us even farther. Remember, then, to focus on how far you have come and don't worry about the speed of your recovery. The ability to love, work, and play will be a good indicator that your recovery is taking place. Hang in there—you'll make it!

QUESTIONS TO ANSWER

1. Who has told you that you will recover?
2. Has your perception of your rape changed? If so, how?

chapter 27

choosing to Heal

*If one advances confidently, in the direction of [her] own dreams,
and endeavors to lead the life [she] has imagined, [she] will meet
with a success unexpected in common hours.*

—Henry David Thoreau

Choosing to heal means going deep inside ourselves. It means we need to change our perception about our trauma. It means taking a hard look at our attitudes. It means we might have to consider forgiveness. Doing all this may be agonizing, temporarily. But healing will come.

Trauma such as rape leaves the psyche deeply wounded, giving Satan an opportunity to step up his attack in the spiritual battle at our weakest front. He picks away at our wound, and the irritation leaves us defiant and defensive with others, and most of all with God. These attitudes of pride and contempt only more deeply wound us by alienating us from those who might support us and help us heal. We perceive hurtful responses from others as meant to further wound us, which serves to further encourage Satan in his spiritual battle.

We cover up our hurt with more attitude or with acting the martyr, but beneath this veneer lies despair. It is desperate to get out and make itself known but is locked in our hearts behind a door of pride and stubbornness.

Neil Anderson, Terry Zuehlke, and Julianne Zuehlke say in their book, *Christ-Centered Therapy*, "Traumatic experiences contribute to the formation of the attitude. They are buried deep in our minds and they are what keep people in bondage to the past; not the traumatic experience itself. The difference is our perception. We cannot undo the reality of what has occurred in our lives, but we do have the power, with the Lord's help, to change the effect that the past may be having on us in current situations."[1]

To change what the past is doing to you now, you need to make a decision. You need to unburden yourself in order to start down the path of healing. You need to lay aside the disappointments and sorrow—some Christians say, "Lay them at the feet of Jesus." Broken dreams and failed beginnings may appear to defeat us, but with Christ, they can never destroy us. You need to trust God for the power for victory over the past.

coping

We can rise from the ashes of our suffering when we realize that sorrow can be a necessary path to our maturity. We cannot always avoid tragedy and despair—nor should we—as they become tests of fire. We can emerge stronger, more confident individuals, or we can give in to our sin nature and accept defeat. If we choose the latter, our past is destined to be our future.

You're reading this book, so on some level you've decided not to give in to defeat. You want to recover. For you to go beyond a recovery that's merely tolerable, though, you must *deal* with your disappointments and sorrow, not just *cope* with them. What's the difference? Coping is like having a burr in your bed and figuring out ways to avoid it; dealing with the burr is removing it so you can get a good night's sleep.

Perhaps you've coped with the past all of your life, putting up a brave front, brushing it off by saying, "It's no big deal." But your past *is* a big deal. You were horribly violated and that needs to be addressed. Coping is simply denying your wounds or minimizing their severity.

Suppose you want a healing that lets you restructure your life. To do that we must learn not merely to cope with disappointments, sorrow, and trauma (even rape), but to deal with them. Denying the severity of your wounds while at the same time using your wounding as an excuse for negative attitudes is not dealing with your trauma. Denying and excusing are just crutches. Breaking the strongholds of your rape experience—that is dealing with it. Dealing with the wound means letting go of anger, bitterness, contempt, and unforgiveness. It means accepting the reality of the past and anticipating that something good will come of it.

Let's say you've come to the point where you're ready to deal with your trauma, ready to stop being angry and bitter. Many rape survivors, though, are still struggling with the big questions: "Why?! Why did this have to happen? Why did it happen to me? Why did God let this happen to me?" Kay Scott writes, "What do we do when we don't understand God's answers? Are we to say, 'God, You are unjust, maybe not righteous after all?' If we do that, then we remove ourselves from God's care; we wall ourselves out at the time of greatest need. We go through life cursing God and His people, rather than finding healing for our hearts even if we cannot gain understanding in our heads."[2]

If you're still struggling with the *Why?* questions, perhaps it's because you want to feel like you have some control: "If I know why, maybe I can do something so it will never happen again." It's natural to want to know why, and perhaps one day you may find out, or at least see how God used the terrible thing that happened to you and brought good out of it. But ask yourself, "Does it makes sense for me to insist I know why before I let God heal me?" Instead of questioning God and cursing His people, try praying this prayer:

Dear God,

I want to begin a new life. Help me turn contempt into contentment, and anger into acceptance. Grace me with a humble spirit, a forgiving heart, and the desire to let you remove my defiant, prideful attitude. Thank You for Your loving-kindness. In Jesus' name, amen.

Forgiveness

Once a survivor of sexual abuse gets past the *Why* questions, her next hurdle is likely to be forgiveness. "I don't like this forgiveness business," you say. "Why should I forgive? My rape tore away part of my life and I will never be the same. Even if I decide I need to forgive, I'm not ready yet to do it."

I know just how you feel. But let's think about it. First, what is forgiveness? What does it mean to forgive?

In *Christ-Centered Therapy*, the authors say, "Forgiving is agreeing to live with the consequences of someone else's sin."[3] The acceptance of our wounded psyche can lead us to grace, forgiveness, love, and compassion. Forgiveness is a matter of the heart, and forgiving is necessary for our souls to rest and be free of the strongholds of pain that are keeping us in bondage. As Lewis Smedes says, "Forgiving is love's revolution against life's unfairness."[4]

Forgiving, though, is not excusing or condoning. Smedes says,

Forgiving does not reduce evil. Forgiving great evil does not shave a millimeter from its monstrous size. When we forgive evil we do not excuse it, we do not tolerate it, and we do not smother it. We look evil full in the face, call it what it is, let its horror shock, stun and enrage us, and only then do we forgive it. If we say that monsters are beyond forgiving, we give them a power they should never have. They are given power to keep their evil alive in the hearts of those who suffered most.

Forgiveness is God's invention for coming to terms with a world in which, despite their best intentions, people are unfair to each other and hurt each other deeply. He began by forgiving us. And He invites us all to forgive each other.[5]

While God wants us to forgive, when we do, it's not for Him— it's for us. It's to set us free and to feel the peace that surpasses all understanding, the kind of peace only God can give. Until we forgive, we cannot escape the strongholds of pain.

Escaping the bondage of pain, though, doesn't mean that we'll never again remember the pain over being raped. Don't confuse forgiveness with forgetting; they are not the same. Forgiveness begins with a decision to forgive, even if we don't feel like it. We do it because it will bring much-needed healing.

Debbie Morris, in her book *Forgiving the Dead Man Walking*, writes,

Our reluctance to forgive is based on the false assumption that forgiving means giving in or giving up something valuable. We think it might mean granting the other person some reward he or she doesn't deserve. Or completely discounting the wrong committed—as if it never happened. That's not how forgiveness works. . . . By forgiving Robert Willie [my perpetrator], I in no way absolved him of his responsibility for what he did to me. So forgiveness isn't giving him anything he doesn't deserve; he gains nothing from it.[6]

She concludes by saying, "Justice didn't do a thing to heal me. Forgiveness did."[7]

Smedes would agree. He said, "You cannot erase the past, you can only heal the pain it has left behind. When you are wronged, that wrong becomes an indestructible reality of your life. When you forgive, you heal your hate for the person who created that reality. But you do not change the facts. And you do not undo all of their consequences. The dead stay dead; the wounded are often crippled still. The reality of evil and its damage to human beings is not magically undone and it can still make us very mad."[8]

We all have people in our lives that we need to forgive. It's easier to forgive someone who has wrecked your car, though, than to forgive someone who has sexually assaulted you. And we must all arrive at the decision to forgive in our own time. Hardened hearts, however, as well as pride, anger, and revenge are attitudes that block the path to forgiveness. God's original plan for humankind didn't include injustice, but we experience it because of sin. We can't escape it.

Forgiveness is not excusing the crime, it is not erasing the wrong of the rapist, nor is it forgetting the pain. Forgiveness is not passive acceptance—letting others stomp on us anytime they wish.

Don't try to figure out how to forgive in your brain; you never will. Smedes said, "When we forgive, we perform a miracle hardly anyone notices. We do it alone; in the private place of our inner selves. We do it silently; no one can record our miracle on tape. We do it invisibly; no one can record our miracle on film. We do it freely; no one can ever trick us into forgiving someone."[9]

We cannot forgive, in fact, at the human level. Smedes is right that forgiveness is a miracle, but it is not *we* who perform it. Rather, it is God who performs the miracle, but only if we let Him. We have to make the decision, though—the courageous choice—to let God help us accept the assault and let go of revenge.

I cannot stand in judgment of those who choose not to do so. I just pray that they will.

God Repairs and Restores

Now you've learned what forgiveness is and what it isn't. Maybe you're ready to forgive. Let's give it a try. Whom do you *choose* to forgive?

If you feel you're not ready, name the main issue that is keeping you from doing so, such as revenge or anger.

If you're not ready to forgive, that's all right . . . for now. Forgiving is a process that takes time; it doesn't happen overnight. Ask God to help you forgive; it's the only way we can do it anyway.

Don't wait too long to make your choice to forgive. Hearts harden—you may never make the decision, thus eliminating your opportunity for wholeness. If you wish to wait for now, write God a letter or poem expressing your resistance, and ask Him to help.

Dear Heavenly Father,
I know You have forgiven me and I in turn need to forgive. But Father, the pain is still so deep, I can't move forward. Guide me in the way of forgiving. Help me to see others through Your eyes so I, too, will show mercy and have the courage to forgive. Amen.

QUESTIONS TO ANSWER

1. Who is telling you that you have a chance to get better? Write down their names. If you can't think of anyone who is encouraging you, where can you go to keep your spirit alive? Write it down.
2. What are you doing to break your isolation? List some ways.
3. What effects of having been raped are holding you in bondage? Write them down. These are the strongholds—the effects—that your rape has on you.
4. How can you change the effects that having been raped has had on you?
5. Identify your type of anger. Is it defiant/prideful, contemptuous, or defensive? How can you overcome your anger?
6. What do you need to accept in order to recover?

signs of Healing

He heals the brokenhearted and binds up their wounds.

—Psalm 147:3

"How will I know if I'm healing?" You might ask this for any number of reasons. You've been hurting for so long, you've forgotten what it feels like not to hurt. Your rape happened a long time ago, but you still think about it and wonder if you ever really recovered. If your rape was more recent, the pain is fresh, but you want to know what to look for in yourself that tells you you're going to be okay. Fill in your own reason.

No matter the reason, though, the very fact that you ask the question means you *want* to recover. And there are many signs that indicate that you *are* recovering. One is that many of your post-traumatic stress symptoms will lessen in frequency and severity— the hyper arousal and anxiety, the nightmares and intrusive memories. Your attitude will change from that of victim to survivor, and you'll have a greater appreciation of life. Your sense of humor will increase. You'll channel your anger and grief into something positive, and your sense of empathy will strengthen.

Other good signs are lack of suicidal thoughts, deriving some meaning from the trauma in your life, fewer panic attacks, being

able to comfort yourself in a nondestructive way, and growth of
self-esteem. You are learning to take your trauma and turn it into
a well of strength.

Recovery involves several elements. You'll experience these elements in no particular order, over no particular time frame, and at
times simultaneously.

mourning

Mourning or grieving means feeling deep pain about something
you have lost. It can be the loss of a loved one or the loss of a physical capability. It can be the loss of a sense of safety in the world. It
often is the loss of certain beliefs about the world.[1]

For a rape survivor, loss means many things in a hundred different ways. Each person is unique and mourns in her own way,
and you've probably already experienced some of the elements
of mourning—the disbelief, anger, bargaining ("if only" state-
ments)—in the aftermath of sexual assault. Mourning is painful,
and but it is necessary in order to arrive at resolution. Mourning
won't last forever, so let yourself mourn because you have, really,
suffered a loss.

Taking Action

Taking action is what you're doing right now. You're seeking information that will enable you to recover from the effects of rape.
Taking action is getting out of bed in the morning, getting dressed,
and pursuing the day.

Taking action is talking to your medical doctor about antidepressants if you suspect you'd benefit from them. The decision to
take antidepressants, however, deserves careful consideration. Pills
need not be the first thing you reach for, and for some people antidepressants are not recommended at all. Your doctor and/or counselor can help you weigh the pros and cons. Above all, spend some
time in prayer before making your decision, telling God why you

think you need medication, what your doctor/counselor has told you about antidepressants, and asking God what He would want you to do.

Acceptance

We live in a fallen world where evil reigns. Bad things happen. Life isn't fair. We need to acknowledge these realities but not let them affect our perceptions of life, people, and God in a negative way. When we can do so, that is acceptance. Adversity strengthens us, instilling confidence to handle crises that may come our way. Despite the pain and devastation that comes with rape, those feelings can guide us toward maturity and inner healing. Something good will come of it.

self-care

Self-care includes making your home and property safe, using common sense about the people you associate with, and parking safely (see also chapter 29). These actions empower you, making you feel like you are in charge. Go back to your normal routine as soon as possible. The normal busyness will crowd out negative mental intrusions.

Resolution

Resolution is firmly deciding to let go of the past and move forward with your life. In the resolution element of recovery, your assault gradually loses its power over you. You are less fearful, your anger has subsided, and you have ceased to blame yourself or others.

Getting to resolution takes time. Don't consider yourself a failure if you feel you haven't "arrived." Let time run its course. Permit yourself to heal gradually. Remember, the more severe the assault, the greater the severity of your secondary wounding, and the less support you have from others, the more time it will take to heal.

Keep in mind, though, that resolution does not remove the

trauma. Your assault happened; that reality will not go away. Resolution is really integration of the other elements of recovery: as you mourn, come to acceptance, practice self-care, and take action to move on with your life, resolution takes hold.

Don't waste your sorrow

There will always be evidence of the scars that result from rape. Memories will linger in the depths of our souls. However, our scars can bear witness to God's unfailing love. He can create new life in us. Our brokenness can cause us to turn our wills and lives over to God. We can give Him our sorrow, and trust that He will make us whole.

Lewis Smedes asks, in his book *Forgive and Forget*, "Will we let our pain hang on to our hearts where it will eat away our joy? Or will we use the miracle of forgiving to heal the hurt we didn't deserve?"[2]

God can help you recover from having been raped. No, He won't undo what has been done, but He can help free you of the strongholds, the negative effects, the rape has had on you. You need to ask Him, though. Ask Him to free you from those strongholds that are keeping you from recovery.

You have a purpose in life. God has a plan for you, and your reason for being is included in that plan. Let God use the pain that has come into your life to help others overcome their pain, to give encouragement, hope, and love. Pray to God for wisdom and understanding:

Dear God,
   Merciful Father God, as I accept my loss and mourn it, help me see where You intervened. Enfold me with understanding. Replace sorrow with joy, and fill me with new love and strength that I may serve You and help others to heal. In Jesus' name, amen.

As time passes and you seek and trust God, your reason for being will most likely be revealed to you.

QUESTION TO ANSWER

What signs indicate recovery coming closer for you?

chapter 29

Taking care of yourself

Time brings understanding and acceptance, so that living becomes meaningful again.

—Laurence J. Peter

Healing involves coming to terms with who you are, learning to see change not as an enemy but as an ally. When you can ask, "How can I find meaning in what has happened in my life?" change becomes possible. What happened in the past will not change. It will not become more beautiful or less ugly. But your feelings in the present—about yourself, about what happened, about what it all means—can change. Healing involves opening up new possibilities, new ways to be in the world that bring more peace inside.[1]

Don't Blame yourself

Many women feel as if they should have done something to avoid being raped. If you could have done something to avoid it, you would have. Believe me, no woman wants to be raped. The very idea is insane. Remember, the rapist is the one who committed the crime, not you.

Don't take the rap for the rapist. And don't let others blame you. They weren't there, and it could just as easily have happened to them.

seek professional help

If you're still having anxiety attacks, long crying spells, prolonged depression, and/or severe anger and rage, please seek professional help. You won't be seen as a "cry baby" or a weakling. Seeking help is a sign of taking care of yourself when you know you've tried everything but recovery is moving along at a snail's pace. Seeking help is taking charge. Counseling can help you move toward recovery.

join an abuse recovery group

Listening and talking with others who've gone through the experience of rape can be very beneficial. You'll feel safe when you share. A combination of individual and group therapy can be powerful.

consider medication

Seek medical consultation if you're having sleep-related problems, depression, panic attacks, or are being overwhelmed by intrusive memories. Today's miracle drugs have few side effects and most are not addictive.

Most likely you'll need medication only for a short time. Medication alone, though, without therapy won't help you resolve your trauma. Neither will therapy alone help if you need the medication. Your doctor and therapist can help you make a decision.

eat healthy and exercise

How you feed your body will determine your mental and physical condition. Treat yourself to a new healthy body. Go to the library or bookstore and find a couple of books on healthy eating. Look at the table of contents. It should include how to recognize food portion sizes (if you want to lose weight or maintain weight) and how to read labels on canned and packaged food. Purchase a calorie counter book—one that lists calories by weight and not just volume—and a food scale, and then spend two weeks weighing your food and counting its calories. It sounds like a lot of work but, believe me, it isn't. After the first two weeks or so, you'll need to weigh only some foods once in a while. Your eye will become trained to recognize portion size. How do you think most of those people in before-and-after magazine ads lost weight? Packaged food: smaller portions, lower calories. Clear your kitchen and refrigerator of all junk food. Read the labels of every prepared food item you buy. It should list not only nutritional values, but ingredients as well. Try to buy those that contain the fewest chemical additives. If possible, buy farm-fresh fruits and vegetables, eggs, and meat, or at least organic foods—especially milk. If you have yard enough, or even a window box, grow your own little vegetable garden, or herb bed. If your zoning allows, raise a few chickens for eggs and meat.

Don't forget to exercise. Ouch! I know you were hoping I wouldn't mention it. But, face it, exercise is important. Walking thirty minutes a day helps keep the pounds away. Not only does exercising burn calories, but it clears the cobwebs from our minds, and helps rid us of anger, tension, and frustration. It's also a great time to pray. Find a walking partner: your neighbor, husband, friend, or your dog.

Keep in mind that the objective is not having a figure that fulfills some arbitrary media or Hollywood ideal. Rather, the goal is a *healthier* mind and body, which will give you a more positive outlook on life and on yourself

Relieve stress

Being raped is a crisis. Crises create stress—in your personal life, in other people's lives, and in your relationships. Stress is difficult to manage, but you can lessen the tension and help yourself feel more at ease. First, stop and consider your present life and how far you've come in your recovery. Count the areas where you've made positive changes: bravery, courage, higher self-esteem, a take-charge attitude, acceptance of yourself and your realities. Consider how much you've let go of anger, bitterness, rage, sadness, and revenge. Taking good care of yourself also means relieving stress. Think about what tactics have worked for you in the past in coping with difficult periods in your life.[2] Among those are probably tears and laughter, which are super stress relievers.

Have a Good Cry

God gave us tears to wash away grief, anger, sorrow, and unanswered questions. Tears are God's way of helping us cope. Tears help to keep our bodies free from disease and restore a sense of balance in our lives. William Shakespeare called our tears "holy water."[3] So for the sake of your health and your sanity, go ahead and have a good sacred sob once in a while.[4]

Have a Good Laugh

God replaces tears with laughter. That is His antidote to tears. When we laugh, our brains release a chemical that naturally restores us. Churches have laughing seminars, and hospitals have laughing rooms—all value humor as healing.

Arland Ussher says, "Humor is the sense of the absurd, which is despair refusing to take itself seriously."[5] Humor and laughter control pain in four major ways: (1) by distracting attention; (2) by reducing tension; (3) by changing expectations; (4) by increasing production of endorphins—the body's natural painkillers. Laughter causes muscle relaxation and is effective for relieving tension.[6] Humor and laughter can reduce emotional pain as well.

Laughter breaks away the fears that cause so many depressions, and can lift one out of the black hole of despondency.

Humor as therapy can have several effects.

- Humor creates a frame of mind that's open to constructive communication with others.

- Humor reduces tension and creates a relaxed atmosphere.
- Humor can lead to insights into the cause of conflict and emotional disturbances.[7]

We need periodic release from the need to be logical and serious about life's responsibilities. Humor allows us to deal in fantasy and nonsense, and find respite from our serious cares and obligations.[8] As the proverb says, "A cheerful heart is good medicine" (17:22).

Here's a prescription for developing a sense of humor.

- Adopt an attitude of playfulness.
- Think funny.
- Laugh at the incongruities in situations involving yourself and others.
- Laugh with others, and not *at* them, and only for what they do rather than for what they are.
- Take yourself lightly.
- Make others laugh.

A sense of humor sees the fun in everyday experiences. It is more important to have fun than it is to be funny.[9]

Enjoy Favorite or New Activities

How about rewarding yourself with a five-minute—or a five-day—retreat? Here are some suggestions for be-good-to-yourself getaways:

- Escape to faraway places in a children's book. When you were child, did your imagination take you to another world in your favorite books? Yes? You can still return—again and again. No? Then now is a good time to start taking imaginary journeys. The enchantment and simplicity of children's books will bring peace and awe into your life.

- Dance to lift your spirits. In spite of what you might think, everyone can dance. No, you don't have to be a professional. Turn up the music and dance to your heart's content. Let the music tell you how to move. It's hard to stay sad when you're dancing.
- Play like a child. Remember all the wonderful games you played as a child? Jacks, paper dolls, tinker toys, jump rope, hopscotch, tag, follow the leader, and hide and seek. Lose yourself in a toy store and surprise yourself with toys to bring home—and play with them!
- Stay at a bed-and-breakfast in your own hometown. There's probably one just around the corner! If not, go to one out of town. If you're on a budget, see if you can stay in your best friend's guest room. The point is to indulge—sleep in someone else's bed, eat their food, dream, and relax.
- Commit yourself to healing. It will come in layers, like new skin growing over a burn. As you deal with each issue of your assault, another layer of healing takes place and the pain becomes less and less.
- Engage in positive self-talk. Tell yourself, "It's possible—not impossible." When you remove negative thoughts, you must fill your mind with positive ones. Filling your mind with Scripture or affirmative quotes is a good idea.
- Go to the library. Silence can be calming. The sights and smells of old books—like old friends—are comforting.
- Work in the garden or the yard. Puttering outside slows down your thoughts and allows your mind to rest.
- Visit garden nurseries. Strolling in a garden center (if you like gardening) focuses your attention on the plants, thereby away from disturbing thoughts.
- Visit a favorite coffeehouse. Hands wrapped around a yummy, hot drink in the winter, or a cold, icy drink in the summer is soothing. It's better than wrapping your hands

around someone's neck (in anger)! Sip a drink, engage in people watching, and relax.

- Soak in the bathtub. A hot or cool (depending on the season) bubble bath can comfort both your body and your mind.
- Learn a new pastime. Try some handiwork such as knitting, crocheting, needlepoint, embroidery, weaving, quilting, or rug hooking. Other options are floral design, calligraphy, writing, painting, doll making, cake decorating, or learning to play a musical instrument. And if you're more daring? Try skydiving, rock climbing, or sailing.
- Befriend an elderly woman. Let her wisdom, knowledge, and wonder seep into you. Volunteer to write letters or run errands for her. Bake cookies together. Buy her a cute pair of jeans—it will make her feel young.
- Tour your own hometown. Discover what others come to see.
- Read comic books . . . but only the funny ones.
- Indulge at your favorite restaurant. Enjoy your favorite food—in moderation.
- Bring the outdoors inside. If you don't have a flower garden, purchase flowers for your office and/or your home. Put them by your bed, in your bathroom, on the kitchen counter, and by your cozy chair.
- Bake bread. Nothing beats the smell of fresh-baked bread. Making it from scratch and kneading it can be relaxing. Tasting the first bite is pure heaven. If you're trying to choose more healthy foods, try making whole wheat or oatmeal bread.
- Take a snooze. Give yourself permission to take a nap. Napping should be a national pastime. A nap restores and refreshes the body, spirit, and mind—and it's free! Don't feel guilty when you lie down; your body is telling you to. The hour you think you've lost will be replaced with a revived

spirit and new energy. A good nap helps remove stress and restores a healthy attitude. So snooze—zzz.

- Get involved in a social group. Increased social activities and social contact provide you with antidotes against intrusive thoughts of your assault. Sign up for a self-defense class. Volunteer to rock babies at your community hospital. Consider being an advocate (when you're ready) for your local sexual assault resource center. If you're busy doing something for someone else, you have less time to dwell on yourself.
- Try deep-breathing exercises. The increased oxygen flow to your brain will increase your ability to think clearly, help with concentration, and rid the body of many toxins. Try this: breathing deeply from your abdomen, inhale slowly to the count of five. Pause and hold your breath to the count of five. Exhale slowly to the count of five. Say the word *relax* three or four times, then repeat the exercise. Do this exercise smoothly and regularly for five minutes.
- Give yourself affirmative pep talks. Continue to tell yourself the rape was not your fault, that you are not afraid, and that you will be victorious.
- Enjoy tranquility. Solitude at times can be lovely. Get up early to watch the sunrise. Prepare the night before by setting out a tray with a linen napkin and a nice cup and saucer. Prepare coffee or tea ahead of time so all you have to do is plug in the pot. Set out fixings for cinnamon toast and fruit. Invite your dog or cat to join you—pets won't ruin the quiet by talking. Then find a front-row seat to enjoy the free, morning-light show. Or do the same for a sunset, enjoying dessert with your great view!
- Purchase humorous books and movies on tape or disk. Audio books are wonderful. Just pop one in your car's player and let the humor tickle you all the way to work, the store,

or wherever you're going. By the time you reach your destination, you'll feel quite chipper. In the evening, wind down with a video comedy, and your body, spirit, and mind will be ready for a good night's sleep. If you need to go cheap, check out tapes and disks from the library.

- Take a break from the ordinary. Rearrange your furniture. Decorate for stress-free living: out with clutter, in with simplicity. Take the long way home (provided the scenery is nice).

- Do something outrageous. Go to the drive-in movies in your jammies. Get a rubber ducky for your bathtub and play with it! Buy a pair of bright yellow or red rubber boots for rainy days, and stomp through water puddles with the neighbor kids. Eat an unfamiliar food item every month. Laugh out loud where strangers can hear you. Believe that you are incredibly resilient—because you are! And live like you are!

- Learn a new "promise Scripture" and tape it to your car's steering wheel. See Exodus 15:26; Psalms 4:8; 57:1; 147:3; Isaiah 41:13; 43:18–19; 55:12; and Jeremiah 29:11.

- Practice affirming yourself. Reject rejection. Smile when you don't want to. Confront conflict. Make mistakes so you can stretch. Love yourself.

- Play the "I Wish" game. Check all of the following that you would wish for. Add a few of your own, and then make one come true.

  I wish I could . . .

  ___ buy or adopt a puppy/kitten.

  ___ take a two-day river cruise.

  ___ take a Chinese cooking class.

  ___ purchase season tickets to the theater or opera.

  ___ join a community theater house.

  ___ take riding/sailing lessons.

_____ climb a mountain.

_____ purchase a teddy bear.

• Read the Bible . . . and count your blessings.

After you've cried again and again over your assault memory, until there are no more tears, start focusing on how far you've come. Remind yourself that you cheated death, you are alive, and you will recover.

QUESTIONS TO ANSWER

1. When was the last time you had a good belly laugh? Can you think of anything funny that happened to you this week? Write it (them) down.

2. What comforting activities can you add to the list in this chapter?

3. Did you do anything last week to comfort yourself?

4. Pick a new comfort for yourself for next week.

chapter 30

Joy will come in the Morning

Forget the former things; do not dwell on the past. See, I am doing a new thing! Now it springs up; do you not perceive it?
—Isaiah 43:18–19

God is the source of all comfort and healing. All the things in the previous chapter that make us feel good and relive stress—they all ultimately come from God. God, the Father of Jesus Christ, the Father of compassion, is the God who comforts us in all our troubles *so we can comfort those in trouble with the same comfort God gave us* (see 2 Cor. 1:3–4).

He knows where you are in times of gladness and in times of sorrow. If you are rising on the wings of the dawn or settling on the far side of the sea, He will guide you and hold you fast. Let God comfort you. Let Him heal you. Dr. Dan Allender says in his book *The Wounded Heart*,

> You have been damaged. But you have great hope. The mercy of God does not eradicate the damage, at least not in this life, but it soothes the soul and draws it forward to a hope that purifies and sets free. Allow the pain of the past and the travail of the change process to create fresh new life

in you and to serve as a bridge over which another victim may walk from death to life. It is an honor beyond compare to be part of the birthing process of life and hope, and a joy deeper than words to see evil and its damage destroyed. I await that day and joy with you.[1]

I, too, await that day and that joy with you. What God did for me, He'll do for you.

Awesome Blessings!

summary steps to wholeness

- Make the choice to heal.
- Allow God to change your perception.
- Let people help; don't isolate yourself.
- Feast on the Word of God.
- Tell your story to a trusted person, get counseling, or both.
- Release your anger, bitterness, contempt, and rage. Write a letter to those who hurt you.
- Find safety in God. Write Him a letter about your hurt.
- Write a letter to yourself from God, having Him console you.
- Mourn. Bring your grief to Jesus, and let Him comfort you.
- Agree to live with the consequences of someone else's sin.
- Take good care of yourself.
- Forgive others.
- Laugh.

When our life of suffering is over, we will be made new. God will wipe every tear from our eyes. There will be no more mourning, crying, pain, or death. Our present suffering is not worth comparing with the coming glory and what God has in store for us (see Rom. 8:18; Rev. 21:3–4).

Dear Daughter,

You've lived in darkness long enough. It's time to put on the armor of light. You are ready to soar like an eagle. Leave sorrow behind. Cast off the chains of fear. Cast off the strongholds of pain. Don't dwell on past mistakes and sorrow.

I'm doing new things in you now. I am healing your broken heart and binding your wounds. I know you don't perceive it now, but as those good and new things spring up, your life will be transformed, and then you will feel My hand upon you.

Don't let evil overcome you. Do good things, overcoming evil with good. I am restoring your health. I am restoring your sanity. I am showering you with peace and prosperity. You will not be afraid anymore. You will dwell in safety and your sleep will be sweet.

I am the God of comfort. I am the Lord, who heals you. Your soul will be filled with joy, and peace will lead you. I am healing your wounds made by thorns and briars. I anoint your spirit with roses and lilies. Come away, My beloved. Let Me continue to heal you.

—God

In the Aftermath of Rape or Sexual Assault

- **Call 911** for help and call a trusted friend, relative, or church leader.
- **Do not** change your clothes (they will be needed for evidence), bathe, brush your teeth, or straighten up the assault area.
- **Go** to the emergency room of a hospital as soon as possible unless the police ask you to wait for them. In that case, they will escort you to the hospital. If you were raped in an unsafe area, let the police know. **When you arrive** at the hospital, most likely an advocate from a sexual assault center will be there for you; you won't be alone. Exams are important to detect injury and inform you of your options regarding pregnancy and protection from sexually transmitted diseases. The state will pay for your exam if police are notified.
- **Report** the crime. Reporting the crime may make you eligible for compensation for medical/counseling costs or losses associated with the crime. Rape is a crime against the state. Reporting the crime will also give you a sense of control, and the information you offer may help prevent the attacker from assaulting again.

205

- **Seek** counseling, preferably with someone who works with sexual assault survivors.
- **Attend** a sexual assault recovery support group. Ask if your church has one.
- **Call** for information on rape crisis services in your community, or check your telephone directory, mental health clinics, local hospital, or police department. Some nonprofit mental health clinics and churches provide counseling for those unable to pay. For more information, call:

Rape, Abuse, and Incest National Network: 800-656-HOPE or http://www.rainn.org/

National Domestic Violence Hotline: 800-799-SAFE or http://www.ndvh.org/

National Suicide Hotline: 800-564-2120

Appendix B

covenant with god

I agree to exchange fear, anger, unforgiveness, and bad choices for love and forgiveness. I will accept change, deal with perceptions, and relent to a teachable spirit. I accept the truth that good will come from bad. I believe God's unfailing love for me. I believe He can free me from the strongholds of the past, thus guiding me to spiritual maturity and wholeness. With God, I believe "awful" is not forever, and that "awesome" will dwell in its place. I will tell my story of healing to others.

Signature   Date

Praise be to the God and Father of our Lord Jesus Christ, the Father of compassion and the God of all comfort, who comforts us in all our troubles, so that we can comfort those in any trouble with the comfort we ourselves have received from God.

—2 Corinthians 1:3–4

A Guide for Husbands, Fathers, and Friends

Facts to Remember

- Rape is a crime of power and control, anger and violence. It is not a crime of passion.
- Survivors did not provoke their rape. The perpetrators are responsible.
- Sexual assault is everyone's problem. We must speak out and break the silence, challenging the social and cultural traditions that nurture it.
- Rape is a crime against the state as well as the survivor.

A Victim's State of Mind

A rape survivor is confused, anxious, and emotionally charged immediately following her rape. She has been terrorized, violated, and is faced with many worries and questions such as the following.

- Should I report this to the police?
- Could I be pregnant?
- Have I contracted venereal diseases or AIDS?
- What will my family, husband, and others think of me?
- Will I ever be the same as before my rape?

- Do I need to see a doctor?
- Will he try to rape me again?

The emotional aftermath of rape continues well beyond the assault. Encouraging the victim to seek medical attention and counseling sends a powerful message that you believe her and view her assault seriously. She will feel your support, knowing she will not have to face her recovery alone.

Because the time following a rape is filled with psychological turmoil, great sensitivity and care must be taken toward the survivor. How you communicate with her is critical. It will contribute to her self-worth. Those closest to her have the honor and power to help her recover.

How You can Help

- Never accuse or judge a rape survivor.
- Don't ask questions such as, "Why didn't you scream for help? Why were you there after dark? Why did you wear that outfit?" Such questions will only make the survivor feel guilty.
- When a woman has been raped, she feels a loss of control over her life. In order to help her regain a sense of control, she should be encouraged to make her own decisions (whether to report the crime, go to trial, etc.).
- Don't demand details of her rape. Be patient. When she is ready to discuss it, she'll let you know.
- She needs to feel your love and know that it will remain intact—that you will endure this crisis together—no matter what happened or will happen later.
- Eventually, you must discuss the impact the rape has had on your relationship. The aftermath of rape is traumatic for everyone involved with the survivor, especially if you are her father, boyfriend, or husband. Nurturing your loved one will speed her recovery.

- Don't joke about or trivialize rape.
- Don't overprotect the survivor. It can discourage her from nurturing coping skills by promoting dependency on others. Help her be independent by supporting her.
- Don't smother her. Accept her need for privacy. It's desirable and therapeutic for her to work alone with her feelings. Well-wishers can often be emotionally draining.
- Take seriously any suicide threat by the rape survivor. Notify her family and counselor immediately.

Additional ways you can help

A rape survivor needs a safe, accepting climate, free of criticism, in order to release painful feelings. Being patient, supportive, and nonjudgmental will send her an important message—that you love her unconditionally. You can help by just being there. Listen, listen, listen.

Protect yourself when you enter into another's pain; it can engulf you. Acknowledge your own inadequacies. You cannot make it better—you have no solutions or answers. Encourage her to seek professional help.

Help her rebuild her internal sense of security. When a woman has been assaulted in her home, her sanctuary can become a constant reminder of that which she wishes to forget.

Don't minimize the assault by saying, "At least you weren't murdered!"

Don't excuse the perpetrator. Assure her the rape was not her fault. There is never an excuse for rape. And for heaven's sake, don't suggest the rape might not have happened if she had prayed harder.

Don't give up on her. Stay for the long haul, because healing is a long process, a lifetime process. She is in a spiritual battle, and Satan is the enemy of her soul and spirit. Don't expect her to fight all by herself. Pray for her. Her faith may feel dead to her in the midst of her darkness, so let her know *you* have faith that her healing will come. Phone occasionally and send notes of encouragement. Invite her to do something fun.

You will find great joy in participating in the restoration of a survivor.

Helping a Friend Work Through Past Assault

What if you suspect your friend has been sexually assaulted in the past? The first step to take is to pray for discernment. Then, gently ask her if she has been sexually abused.

Sometimes, she may answer *no*. It may take time for her to gain trust in you. She may have never told anyone. When she does confide, encourage her to share all her feelings, emotions, and thoughts about it. Assure her of privacy, and then *keep your promise*. Never share with anyone, not even your spouse (unless you have permission), what a survivor of assault has shared with you in confidence. The exception is reporting suicide threats. Call 911 immediately so the person can be placed in a hospital for observation.

When she opens up to you, be kind. Encourage her. Let her know she doesn't have to live in darkness, that God is a God of comfort who binds up wounds and heals broken hearts (Ps. 147:3). He restores fractured minds and sick bodies, and will bring her the peace she has longed for.

Show her God's promises in the Scriptures, such as "I am the LORD who heals you" (Ex. 15:26). Encourage her to embrace one Scripture that especially speaks to her, to memorize it, and say it aloud when old negative thoughts or depression surface. Suggest she carry it in her purse, tape it to her car steering wheel and bathroom mirror, and tuck it under her pillow. But don't insist on it. She may feel pressured and back away. Allow her as much time as needed.

Listen to your friend as she tells her story and speaks of her pain. A woman once said to me, "You talk too much!" when I was trying to be helpful. I was mildly annoyed at her remark (okay, I was

very annoyed). Later, over time, I swallowed my pride and agreed
... she was right. I learned I needed to speak less and *listen* more.
And by listening prayerfully to the pain of another, we can hear the
Holy Spirit speaking to us, and therefore know how to react in the
correct way.

Listening quietly speaks loudly to the one bearing her soul.
Patricia Weaver Francisco says in her book *Telling*, "When a soul is
lost, it is in need of others. This is what we mean by help—a listening ear, a place to rest."[1] Just maintain attention by looking at your
friend as she talks, and when she makes eye contact nod your head
occasionally to encourage her and let her know you are focused on
her.

When a woman in pain breaks down sobbing, hand holding
and hugging may *sometimes* send a negative message: "You're okay,
you're going to be all right, now, let's move along." She doesn't *always*
need a hug, or her hand held, but she does need a listening ear. We
must learn the difference.

If, over time, there seems to be very little or no progress in your
friend's recovery, suggest professional counseling, someone quali-
fied in helping rape survivors. She may also want to attend a rape/
sexual assault recovery group. In combination, these are powerful
tools for healing.

Remember, healing comes gradually. For some, it can take a lifetime. Survivors have to adapt to being new people. They don't view
the world the same as they did before their assault. Rape changes
their perception of life. If your friend feels progress isn't taking
place, encourage her to see how far she has come; have her count
the ways. Tell her not to worry about the speed of her healing, but
that she *will* recover.

God is the source of all comfort and healing. God, the Father of
Jesus Christ, the Father of compassion, is the God who comforts us
in all our troubles so we can *comfort those in trouble with the same
comfort God gave us* (see 2 Cor. 1:3–4).

Dear church

Candace Walters, in her book *Invisible Wounds*, writes an open letter to the church:

> The church as a whole is ignorant, unprepared, and oblivious to the problem of sexual assault. Satan has taken advantage of the church's uninvolvement to continue to attack Christians and non-Christians alike.
>
> Additionally, the Christian community is almost wholly neglectful in teaching girls and women rape awareness and prevention. This gives church women a false sense of security and a harder time dealing with an actual assault. Some professionals feel that the number of persons in the Christian community who are victims of sexual abuse is extremely high because the church is naïve thus vulnerable.
>
> The church produces a sad predicament for the victim of sexual violence. Most pastors say they rarely or never have had a rape victim come to them for counsel. Because sexual assault is so extensive, they agree it was not because few church women were involved, but because the victim does not ask them for help. She senses, often correctly, that the collective church would respond to her with awkwardness and inappropriate assistance.

Would churches then be receptive to a presentation to better understand the problem? A number of pastors say no. Because few victims have come forth, the clergy concludes it is not a concern within their congregation. Rape is a crime against God and humanity. The body of Christ is called to express God's love and healing to anyone experiencing grief and pain. Pastors and lay people need to recognize the rape victim as an individual who deserves their most compassionate and educated response. As salt of the earth, Christians have a unique opportunity and God-given responsibility to stem evil wherever it abounds. Apathy and ignorance give women the impression that sexual violence is the unmentionable sin.[1]

While many pastors would like to help rape victims, they don't know how. Rape counseling is something most pastors do not learn in seminary. They agree it would be better to help survivors in the church family, but few churches offer this service.

In addition, churches often mistrust secular rape counseling services. Likewise, rape crisis centers are skeptical of the ability of the church, as most have remained uninformed and uninvolved. The truth is both secular and spiritual resources are beneficial. But if women are not given an option of spiritual counseling, they may not seek help at all.

The church can encourage advocates to take training in rape awareness, prevention, and recovery. The congregation can then be made aware that people are ready to help. The church can provide a loving, nonjudgmental atmosphere as the survivor accepts answers to her pain and receives prayer for restoration—something she would not receive in a secular setting.

It's time to pray that the church will become involved in setting the rape captive free—free to be a vibrant survivor instead of a defeated victim.

suggested Reading

Allender, Dan B. *The Wounded Heart* (Colorado Springs, CO: NavPress, 1990). For adult survivors of childhood sexual abuse. A must read for incest survivors.

Cloud, Henry, and John Townsend. *Boundaries* (Grand Rapids: Zondervan, 1992). When to say yes, when to say no. Learn to take control of your life.

Emmons, Freda. *Flame of Healing* (Mustang, OK: Tate, 2006). A daily journey of healing from abuse and trauma.

Hurnard, Hannah. *Hinds' Feet on High Places* (Wheaton, IL: Tyndale, 1977). An allegory of hope and courage when faced with fear.

Langberg, Diane Mandt. *On the Threshold of Hope* (Wheaton, IL: Tyndale, 1999). Healing sexual abuse. A gentle book full of hope and God's grace.

Ledray, Linda E. *Recovering from Rape* (New York: Henry Holt, 1994). In-depth information about rape and how to recover.

Masteller, James, and David Stoop. *Forgiving Our Parents: Forgiving Ourselves* (Grand Rapids: Zondervan, 1991). Forgiving your parents.

Meyer, Joyce. *Beauty for Ashes* (New York: Time Warner Faith, 1994). How to recover from the pain of mental, emotional, and sexual abuse.

New Beginnings: Daily Devotions for Women Survivors of Sexual Abuse (Nashville: Thomas Nelson, 1992). Out of print but worth looking for.

Savard, Liberty. *Shattering Your Strongholds* (Gainesville, FL: Bridge Logos, 1992). How to break the strongholds of wrongful thinking.

Smedes, Lewis B. *Forgive and Forget* (New York: Pocket Books, 1984). How to forgive.

Notes

chapter 1: Nighttime Intruder

1. Frederick Buechner, *Godric* (New York: Atheneum, 1981), 51.
2. Willard Trask, *Joan of Arc: In Her Own Words* (New York: Turtlepoint, 1996), 4–5.

chapter 4: The Loud, Silent Year

1. Trevor Hudson, *Christ Following* (Grand Rapids: Baker, 1996), 67.
2. Liberty Savard, *Shattering Your Strongholds* (Gainesville, FL: Bridge Logos, 1992), 90.
3. Neil Anderson, Terry Zuehlke, and Julianne Zuehlke, *Christ-Centered Therapy* (Grand Rapids: Zondervan, 2000), 156.

chapter 6: Perpetrators Change—Well, Some Do

1. Used by permission.

chapter 7: Tough Love

1. Gavin de Becker, *The Gift of Fear* (New York: Dell, 1997), 56.
2. Used by permission.

chapter 8: God can create new Life

1. Bruce Larson, *Living Beyond Our Fears* (New York: Harper-Collins, 1990).
2. Luis Palau, *Where Is God When Bad Things Happen?* (New York: Doubleday, 1999), 215–16.

chapter 9: original Trauma

1. Candace Walters, *Invisible Wounds* (Portland, OR: Multnomah, 1987), 47.
2. Aphrodite Matsakis, *I Can't Get Over It* (Oakland, CA: New Harbor, 1986), 85.
3. Mariann Hybels-Steer, *Aftermath* (New York: Fireside, 1995), 29.
4. Ibid., 35.

chapter 10: Fear and the Loss of safety

1. Linda E. Ledray, *Recovering from Rape* (New York: Henry Holt, 1994), 11.
2. Nancy Vanable Raine, *After Silence* (New York: Crown, 1998), 80.
3. Benjamin Colodzin, *How to Survive Trauma* (Barrytown, NY: Station Hill, 1992), 19–20.
4. Ibid, 20–21.

chapter 11: Post-Traumatic stress

1. Colodzin, *How to Survive Trauma*, 1–2.
2. Diane Langberg, *On the Threshold of Hope* (Wheaton, IL: Tyndale, 1999), 108.
3. Sean Mactire, *Malicious Intent* (Cincinnati, OH: Writer's Digest, 1995), 134.
4. Ibid., 134, 138.

chapter 12: Depression

1. Herbert Wagemaker, *The Surprising Truth About Depression* (Grand Rapids: Zondervan, 1994), 123.
2. Ibid., 177.
3. Colodzin, *How to Survive Trauma*, 33–34.
4. Ibid., 34–35.
5. Ibid., 36–37.

chapter 13: shame and Guilt

1. *Oxford American Dictionary* (New York: Avon Books, 1980), s.v. "Shame."
2. Michael Lewis quoted in Raine, *After Silence*, 131.
3. Willard Gaylin, *Adam & Eve & Pinocchio* (New York: Viking Penguin, 1990), 85.
4. Lewis B. Smedes, *Shame and Grace* (New York: HarperCollins, 1993), 96.
5. *Oxford American Dictionary* (New York: Avon Books, 1980), s.v. "Guilt."

chapter 15: Memories

1. Carl Jung as quoted in Mactire, *Malicious Intent*, 30.
2. George Johnson, *In the Palaces of Memory* (New York: Alfred A. Knopf, 1991), xi, xiv, 230, 232–33.
3. Colodzin, *How to Survive Trauma*, 87.

chapter 16: writing to Heal

1. Eddie Ensley and Robert Hermann, *Writing to Be Whole* (Chicago: Loyola Press, 2001), x.
2. Louise DeSalvo, *Writing as a Way of Healing* (San Francisco: HarperCollins, 1999), 25.
3. Ensley and Hermann, *Writing to Be Whole*, 7.
4. Used by permission.

chapter 17: secondary wounding

1. Walters, *Invisible Wounds*, 86.
2. Ledray, *Recovering from Rape*, 103–5.

chapter 18: they do it because they want to

1. Mactire, *Malicious Intent*, 32.
2. Ibid., 34.
3. Ibid., 25, 34.
4. Ibid., 2–25 passim.
5. According to the United Nations' Office of Drug and Crime, 95,136 rapes were committed in America in 2001–2002, giving the United States the highest rape count in the world. And these are only the reported ones ("The Eighth United Nations Survey of Crime Trends and Operations of Criminal Justice Systems [2001–2002]," available at http://www.unodc.org/unodc/en/data-and-analysis/Eighth-United-Nations-Survey-on-Crime-Trends-and-the-Operations-of-Criminal-Justice-Systems.html).
6. Liz Kelly, *Surviving Sexual Violence* (Minneapolis: University of Minnesota Press, 1988), 199.
7. Marc MacYoung and Dianna Gordon MacYoung, "Profile of a Rapist," No Nonsense Self-Defense LLC, http://www.nononsenseselfdefense.com/profile.html. Used by permission.
8. Robert R. Hazelwood, "Sexual Violence: Perpetrators and Victims" (seminar, Portland, OR, 1997). The information can also be found in Robert R. Hazelwood and Ann Wolbert Burgess, *Practical Aspects of Rape Investigation: A Multidisciplinary Approach*, 3rd ed. (Boca Raton, FL: CRC Press, 2001).
9. Linda S. Mintle, "Marital Rape Is Real," http://www.cbn.com/LivingTheLife/Features/DrLindaHelps/MaritalRape.aspx.
10. Dari K. Sweeton, "Healing the Trauma of Rape," http://www.ecounseling.com/articles/684.

chapter 19: where's god?

1. Walters, *Invisible Wounds*, 88.
2. Larry Crabb, *Connecting* (Nashville: Word, 1997), 31, 53, 127, 170.
3. Walters, *Invisible Wounds*, 90.
4. Used by permission.

chapter 20: Relationship Effects

1. Patricia Weaver Francisco, *Telling: A Memoir of Rape and Recovery* (New York: HarperCollins, 2000), 206.

chapter 22: Mother Eve

1. E. F. Harrison and Charles F. Pfeiffer, eds., *The Wycliffe Bible Commentary* (Chicago: Moody, 1962), 1.
2. Ibid., 5.
3. *Zondervan NIV Matthew Henry Commentary* (Grand Rapids: Zondervan, 1992), 7.
4. Harrison and Pfeiffer, *Wycliffe*, 6.
5. Ibid., 5.
6. Ellen G. White, *The Great Controversy: Between Christ and Satan* (Mt. View, CA: Pacific Press, 1888), 541.

chapter 23: A social and cultural crisis

1. Rachel Biale, *Women and the Jewish Law* (Brooks, NY: Schocken, 1984), 27.
2. "Painful Memories from China's Foot Binding Survivors," www.sfmuseum.org/chin/foot.html.
3. Sandra MacKey, *The Saudis: Inside the Desert Kingdom* (New York: Signet, 1990), 142.
4. Rape, Abuse, and Incest National Network, http://www.rainn.org/statistics.

5. Both the fourth Geneva Convention and Protocols I and II to the Geneva Conventions explicitly prohibit rape.

6. "Crime Statistics," http://www.cityrating.com/citycrime.asp? city=Las+Vegas&state=NV

7. Patricia Tjaden and Nancy Thoennes, "Extent, Nature, and Consequences of Rape Victimization: Findings from the National Violence Against Women Survey." National Institute of Justice and the Centers for Disease Control and Prevention (2006).

8. Ibid.

9. "Nearly six out of ten sexual assault incidents are reported by victims to have occurred in their own home or at the home of a friend, relative, or neighbor." "Sex Offenses and Offenders: An Analysis of Data on Rape and Sexual Assault," Bureau of Statistics, Office of Justice Programs, U.S. Department of Justice (1997).

10. "Approximately 73 percent of rape victims know their assailants." Rape, Abuse, and Incest National Network, http://www.rainn.org/statistics.

11. "It's In Our Hands: Stop Violence Against Women," Amnesty International Report, July 10, 2006, available at Disabled Women's Network Ontario, http://dawn.thot.net/right_of_choice.html.

12. Walters, *Invisible Wounds*, 26. A couple years ago I asked Candice Walters if she thought church and societal views of rape had changed. She replied, "Very little." Domestic violence and sexual assault coalitions often write of incidents where society holds on to antiquated views of sexual assault and sexual assault victims.

13. Ibid., 29.

14. "Ibrahim Abdullahi, a spokesperson for the Societal Reorientation Directorate, a group tasked with improving morals in Kano, said some rapists think they can cure themselves of

HIV and other STDs by having sex with a virgin. Others believe that child rape is a ritual that can lead to instant wealth." "Child Rape on the Rise in North Nigerian City," *Agence France Presse*, January 3, 2008, http://www.aegis.com/news/ads/2008/AD080024.html.

15. "Myths About Rape," Kansas State University Women's Center, www.k-state.edu/womenscenter/. Statistics from U.S. Department of Justice, http://www.ojp.usdoj.gov/bjs/abtract/soo.htm, and Rape Assistance and Awareness Program, http://www.raap.org/ststas.htm.

16. "It's In Our Hands," Amnesty International Report, http://dawn.thot.net/right_of_choice.html.

chapter 24: victim thinking

1. "Constructing a Leaded Glass Panel," http://www.thestore finder.com/glass/library/leaded_glass.htm.

2. Vicki Aranow and Monique Lang, *Journey to Wholeness* (Holmes Beach, FL: Learning Publications, 2001), 114.

3. Walters, *Invisible Wounds*, 89, 97.

chapter 25: Releasing Your Anger

1. Used by permission.

2. Walters, *Invisible Wounds*, 95.

3. Ibid., 96.

chapter 26: Do We Ever Recover?

1. Ronald Bassman, "Overcoming the Impossible," *Psychology Today* (January/February 2001): 39.

chapter 27: Choosing to Heal

1. Anderson, Zuehlke, and Zuehlke, *Christ-Centered Therapy*, 97.

2. Kay Scott, *Sexual Assault* (Grand Rapids: Bethany, 1993), 103.

3. Anderson, Zuehlke, and Zuehlke, *Christ-Centered Therapy*, 156.
4. Lewis B. Smedes, *Forgive and Forget* (New York: Pocket Books, 1984), 107.
5. Ibid., 112.
6. Debbie Morris with Gregg Lewis, *Forgiving the Dead Man Walking* (Grand Rapids: Zondervan, 1998), 249.
7. Ibid., 251.
8. Smedes, *Forgive and Forget*, 1.
9. Ibid., 191.

chapter 28: signs of Healing
1. Hybels-Steer, *Aftermath*, 108.
2. Smedes, *Forgive and Forget*, 21.

chapter 29: Taking care of Yourself
1. Colodzin, *How to Survive Trauma*, 14.
2. Aranow and Lang, *Journey to Wholeness*, 75.
3. William Shakespeare, *King Lear*, act 4, scene 3, line 30.
4. Sue Augustine, *5-Minute Retreats for Women* (Eugene, OR: Harvest House, 2001), 72.
5. Arland Ussher quoted in Laurence J. Peter and Bill Dana, *The Laughter Prescription* (New York: Ballantine Books, 1982), 73.
6. Peter and Dana, *Laughter Prescription*, 73.
7. Ibid., 8.
8. Ibid., 77.
9. Ibid., 193.

chapter 30: Joy will come in the Morning
1. Dan B. Allender, *The Wounded Heart* (Colorado Springs, CO: NavPress, 1990), 263.

Appendix c: A Guide for Husbands, Fathers, and Friends

1. Francisco, *Telling*, 206.

Appendix D: Dear church

1. Walters, *Invisible Wounds*, 116–18.

About the Author

Leila Rae Sommerfeld holds an Advanced Certificate in Pastoral Care to Women from Western Seminary in Portland, Oregon, and is a member of the American Association of Christian Counselors. She spent countless hours helping sexually assaulted women through the steps of recovery as a former volunteer counselor at Good Samaritan Ministries and advocate of the Washington County Sexual Assault Resource Center. Leila now teaches Taking Back Control, an eighteen-hour seminar for women seeking recovery from the aftermath of rape, and is in training to become a life-purpose coach.

Leila lives in Gresham, Oregon, with her husband. They have three daughters, seven grandchildren, and one great-granddaughter.

To share your story or seek seminar information, contact the author via her Web site, http://www.leilarae.com. She would be delighted to hear from you.

Also by the author

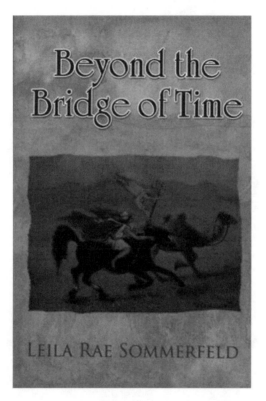

Beyond the
Bridge of Time

LEILA RAE SOMMERFELD

Hadia's anger and unforgiveness toward her father's murderers, her dying mother's secret, and men in general left her seriously doubting God's unfailing love for her. While on her search for the ancient Garden of Eden, a mysterious man name Jude appears to Hadia, offering to guide her and her troop across the Valley of Tremble. He seems to know all about her. On the trail to Paradise Hadia surrenders her heart to God after seeing love and forgiveness in action. Hope found its way into her heart, changing her forever.